The
I Found It!
Series

POWER AND PRAYERS TO NEUTRALIZE LEVIATHAN

ENDING THE SIEGE OF THE DEMON OF THE WATERS AND SEAS

JOSHUA TAYO OBI-GBESAN

xulon
PRESS

To the Good Shepherd who has empowered and sustained me by His Spirit to go forth and set at liberty those who are agonizing under Satanic yokes and oppression

Acknowledgments

First and foremost, I give glory and honor to the Lord who empowered me, by the Holy Spirit, to compile this handbook.

Unending thanks to my lovely wife, Marion B. Obi-gbesan, for her support, perseverance, and ceaseless words of encouragement...

My sincere appreciation for the prayer support and backing of Apostle Samuel A. Sotade and the ministers and members of Mountain of Fire and Miracles Ministries (Colorado, U.S. Branch)...

My special thanks also to Donna Scuderi, who was divinely connected to undertake the rigors of editing and correcting the manuscript...

And grateful acknowledgment to my father in the Lord, the dynamic General Overseer of the Mountain of Fire and Miracles Ministries worldwide, Dr. Daniel K. Olukoya, whose boundless gift of writing has influenced my writing of this book.

Contents

Introduction

The Leviathan Demon

Proverbs 4:7 gives very strong advice to all who purpose to live the victorious life. It says *"Wisdom is the principal thing; therefore get wisdom: and with all thy getting get understanding."*

The Holy Spirit charges, with all purpose and intention, that a believer in Christ Jesus *must* get spiritual understanding. A believer devoid of this understanding will commit spiritual errors that may keep him bound and oppressed.

In fact, the first verse in Proverbs chapter 4 tells us to *"... attend to know understanding."* By this, the Holy Spirit charges us to purposefully acquire spiritual understanding of what is behind the events and issues in our lives.

As a deliverance minister, God has given me the grace to conduct deliverance ministrations and counseling in many churches. Through such ministrations, I have become acquainted with many of the challenges confronting the true Church of Christ, her ministers, and her members. There are strange conflicts in the Church; strange misunderstandings, divisions, envy, and strife; strange attacks against finances and business ventures; and many other strange happenings ranging from spiritual stagnation to spiritual compromise.

I therefore purposed to receive from the Holy Spirit greater understanding of the war being waged against the Church. My quest was fueled by the conviction that a particular demon was linked to some of the problems and struggles I had witnessed, even in our church. We saw the efforts of this demon to afflict members and fragment the congregation—but by the power in the blood of Jesus Christ, his purposes have been thwarted!

As I engaged myself in serious prayer concerning these issues, I had a dream in which I was standing alone inside a big, beautiful church auditorium. Suddenly, a little white bird flew in from the south end of the sanctuary and landed a few yards away from where I stood. The white bird lowered itself and laid a white egg on the floor. Immediately, the bird flew out through the north end of the auditorium.

Just then and from out of nowhere appeared a giant creature at the auditorium's east end. He walked straight toward the just-laid egg and swallowed it. He then turned and walked away without paying me any mind at all.

It was then that I awoke. Many thoughts came to mind. My first thought about the dream was that something *brought forth* (that is, the small, white bird brought forth an egg) and another *swallowed up* (that is, the monster devoured the egg).

By divine impression, I realized that the little white bird represents the Holy Spirit and the white egg symbolizes the blessings the Spirit brings forth. The giant creature is a demonic entity whose assignment it is to devour the blessings God intends for His people to enjoy.

Upon receiving this revelation, it became clear that the Holy Spirit was guiding me into an understanding of this demonic entity's activities. The Holy Spirit connected me to the Book of Job, chapter 41 where the Lord exposes a demonic entity named *Leviathan.*

According to Pastor Win Worley of Hegewisch Baptist Church in Highland, Indiana, "Leviathan resides in the holy place and is a counterfeiter."[1] Further, Leviathan is a principality demon specifically commissioned to stand against God's good plan for His children and destroy the Body of Christ.

A good understanding of the activities of this wicked demon and sound knowledge as to the kind of warfare to be raised against him in prayer will ensure victory over him and his master, Satan.

The successes we have experienced against the Leviathan spirit form the foundation of the spiritual, yet practical teaching you are about to receive.

Endnote

1. Win Worley, *Smashing the Hosts of Hell*, (Highland, IN: Hegewisch Baptist Church, 1993), 26.

Chapter 1

Leviathan's Attack on the Church

As the coming of our Lord Jesus Christ draws near, the principal demon called Leviathan will manifest more violently against the Church of God and His children. What we are seeing in these days are signs that the day of the Lord is near.

The attack that is already unleashed against the Church of God has so weakened her that many live in the shadow of "old glories," having lost the lively tempo of spiritual growth experienced early in the Christian walk and having accepted the condition of stunted spirituality. They have become so passive that prayer and fasting are no longer used as powerful God-ordained weapons to still the hands of the enemy. This attack has reduced churches to social gatherings where fashion is on display and messages from the pulpit spur emotional reaction without spawning genuine spiritual impact.

This attack has hardened the hearts of men and women. There is no longer the experience of genuine repentance in the Church. Many believers are no longer spiritually touched by the errors they commit in their daily lives. Abominable things are done without remorse or regard to the judgment of God. The attacks of the principal demon Leviathan have produced a passive and dead Church.

The attack already unleashed against genuine believers in Jesus Christ has wreaked havoc in their marriages, families, relationships, businesses, finances, careers, educations, callings, ministries, and in their ability to serve the Lord in spirit and in truth. For many, this attack has so fragmented their lives that they entertain suicidal thoughts.

However, our Lord Jesus Christ has given us boldness by His Word in the Gospel of St. John:

> *These things I have spoken unto you, that in me ye might have peace. In the world ye shall have tribulation: but be of good cheer; I have overcome the world* (John 16:33).

Because He has overcome, we as believers in Him have also overcome all things that stand contrary to us and to His kingdom. We can do all things through Him who strengthens us (see Phil. 4:13). Amen!

Often, when the Lord speaks, He speaks in words or parables that are encoded with truth. The Holy Spirit is the One who decodes these words or parables for the children of the living God. God also uses symbols, signs, or characters to speak to us. The Book of Hosea reveals this method of revelation used by God in instructing His people:

> *I have also spoken by the prophets, and I have multiplied visions,* **and used similitudes,** *by the ministry of the prophets* (Hosea 12:10, emphasis added).

Similitudes are comparisons of items that bear spiritual resemblance. God uses them to speak to His people. For example, when He desires to expose wickedness in humans or spirits, He often does so by referring to animals or birds. The Lord did this when He spoke to the Prophet Ezekiel:

> *Son of man, set thy face against Pharaoh king of Egypt, and prophesy against him, and against all Egypt: speak, and say, Thus saith the Lord GOD; Behold, I am against thee,* **Pharaoh king of Egypt, the great dragon that lieth in the midst of his rivers,** *which hath said, My river is mine own, and I have made it for myself* (Ezek. 29: 2-3, emphasis added).

Here, the Lord referred to Pharaoh, ruler of Egypt, as the great dragon. The character and activities of Pharaoh were revealed in the Lord's description of the character and activities of the water dragon.

Similarly, Jesus called Herod the tetrarch a fox. Jesus spoke of the kind of demon that possessed Herod; it was a demon having the character and attributes of a fox. The fox eats the flesh to survive and thereby must shed blood. Herod the tetrarch shed blood in order to stay in power.

The same day there came certain of the Pharisees, saying unto him, Get thee out, and depart hence: for Herod will kill thee. And he said unto them, Go ye, and tell that fox, Behold, I cast out devils, and I do cures today and tomorrow, and the third day I shall be perfected (Luke 13:31-32).

When the Lord appeared to Job to instruct him, He revealed to Job a terrible and wicked demon; He depicted it as a water monster similar to, but not identical to, a single earthly species. This demon presents itself in a variety of ways. For example, it could appear crocodile-like in one instance and whale-like in another, yet never fully resembling either creature. The Lord was very clear, however, about the demon's name: it is *Leviathan* (see Job 41).

Books have been written about this deadly spirit who is so powerful that only God can contain him. This demonic monster has his habitation in the waters and the seas.

Demons often transform into spiritual animals to attack their victims. The changing appearance of the Leviathan spirit is pegged to the purpose of his attack. He can embark on a mission to swallow, bite, sting, strangulate, destroy, or kill. He also embarks on missions to oppress or possess. The Bible speaks of his many heads:

Thou breakest the heads of leviathan in pieces, and gavest him to be meat to the people inhabiting the wilderness (Psalms 74:14).

With his many heads, Leviathan transforms into different kinds of animals that perform specific evil deeds.

Even before the Lord specifically named Leviathan in Job 41, Job appears to have had some insight into the monster demon that had been loosed against him by Satan. In speaking about the power of God, Job spoke of Leviathan as the "crooked serpent" as in Job 26:13:

> By his spirit he hath garnished the heavens; his hand hath formed the crooked serpent (Job 26:13).

Based on this verse, I believe that Job was aware of Leviathan early on. However, it is also clear that Job would gain a clearer understanding concerning the wicked and violent water demon as the Lord exposed Leviathan more fully in Job 41.

Remember, Leviathan takes on different forms as needed. The Holy Spirit revealed Leviathan as a "crooked serpent" (see Job 26:13; Isa. 27:1) and as a "piercing serpent" (see Isa. 27:1). Leviathan presents himself as a crooked serpent when he purposes to swallow or strangulate. He transforms into a piercing serpent when he purposes to bite or sting.

By the Holy Spirit, the prophet Isaiah also qualified Leviathan as *"the dragon that is in the sea"*:

> In that day the LORD with his sore and great and strong sword shall punish leviathan the piercing serpent, even leviathan that crooked serpent; and he shall slay the dragon that is in the sea (Isa. 27:1).

The term *dragon* is common in Scripture and is typically suggestive of Satan, the king of all demons and the father of all wicked acts. Because Isaiah refers to Leviathan as a dragon, we recognize in the water demon the character and abilities of Satan (the dragon of the air).

In Job Chapter 41, the Lord exposes the Leviathan spirit at some length. All disclosures of this spirit reveal a water monster that is somewhat crocodile-like or even whale-like, yet not entirely one or the other. The Leviathan demon has the ability to transform into a creature that resembles a known animal, yet is not that animal. In other words, he is able to obscure his identity so that when he attacks, he is not easily recognized.

Leviathan's Anatomy Revealed by the Lord

Canst thou draw out leviathan with a hook? or his tongue with a cord which thou lettest down? Canst thou put an hook into his nose? or bore his jaw through with a thorn? (Job 41:1-2).

The Lord tells us in the first verse of the above passage that Leviathan seeks to hide. His habitation (the sea) is his hiding place. The sea is also his defense. He must be brought out of the sea in order for the Lord's weapons to be used against him and destroy him.

According to the Lord's words to Job, neither human effort nor strength can prevail over the demon called Leviathan. The Lord says that Leviathan is too proud to surrender to anybody, except with the Lord's backing.

Will he make many supplications unto thee? will he speak soft words unto thee? Will he make a covenant with thee? wilt thou take him for a servant for ever? (Job 41:3-4).

This stubborn principality cannot be appeased. He is so fierce that anyone who has an encounter with him is afraid to do so again. Only the Spirit-filled believer can stand up to and against Leviathan, in the name of Jesus.

Lay thine hand upon him, remember the battle, do no more (Job 41:8).

Leviathan is difficult to uncover. His facial appearance is not easily known as a particular monster.

Who can discover the face of his garment? or who can come to him with his double bridle? Who can open the doors of his face? his teeth are terrible round about (Job 41:13-14).

Spiritually speaking, this demon is revealed as one that can withstand strong counterattack. The Lord explained that Leviathan has a protective covering that is not easily penetrated. Scripture also reveals that the outer part of Leviathan is the pride of his defense. This outer part serves as a kind of bullet-proof covering.

His scales are his pride, shut up together as with a close seal. One is so near to another, that no air can come between them. They are joined one to another, they stick together, that they cannot be sundered (Job 41:15-17).

This is one of the reasons why anyone who comes under the attack of Leviathan can only resist and overcome him by the power of the Holy Ghost and the blood of Jesus.

The Lord also reveals the character of Leviathan. God's Word says that Leviathan's heart is as solid as a stone. Once he decides to strike, he does not change his mind. In other words, Leviathan is stubborn and set in his own ways.

His heart is as firm as a stone; yea, as hard as a piece of the nether millstone (Job 41:24).

Leviathan's hard, uncompromising heart is filled with pride. He is referred to by God as a king of the prideful.

He beholdeth all high things: he is a king over all the children of pride (Job 41:34).

There was a time during his reign as king of Babylon that Nebuchadnezzar was possessed by the Leviathan spirit, as revealed by his prideful words:

Is not this great Babylon, that I have built for the house of the kingdom by the might of my power, and for the honour of my majesty? (Dan. 4:30).

The Bible says Nebuchadnezzar's heart was lifted up; his mind was hardened in pride until the Lord dealt with him by removing his glory from him.

But when his heart was lifted up, and his mind hardened in pride, he was deposed from his kingly throne, and they took his glory from him (Dan. 5:20).

Leviathan is a fierce opponent of God's kingdom. We have seen that he appears in many spiritual disguises. We have also seen that his attacks come in many forms. Pride is one the most insidious and damaging weapons of his warfare against the Church of Jesus Christ.

Chapter 2

Leviathan's Weapons of Warfare

The Lord exposes the weapons found in the arsenal of the Leviathan spirit.

I will not conceal his parts, nor his power, nor his comely proportion (Job 41:12).

The Lord separates Leviathan's weapons into three categories: his physical parts, his power, and his body structure. These are the power secrets of the Leviathan spirit.

Leviathan's physical parts are the body parts through which specific attacks are carried out. These parts can be likened to instruments by which evils are launched.

When we speak of Leviathan's power, we refer to his inherent ability to achieve wicked aims through the forces of wickedness that are released via his body parts. His power includes his stamina, which is his capability to resist counterattack.

Leviathan's "comely proportion" refers to his massive body, which is reinforced with scales that are tightly fixed together. These scales are superb instruments of defense and intimidation.

Just as earthly military forces conduct a range of activities related to warfare, so does the Leviathan demon. These activities include surveillance (the monitoring of opponents' activities), defensive measures (taken in response to opponents' aggression or threats of aggression), and the weapons of attack (offensive measures that initiate battles).

Leviathan's Physical Parts Are Weapons

Leviathan's body parts are weapons used for monitoring and for attack. These include his eyes, tongue, mouth, nose and teeth Let's examine them more closely.

His Eyes

> ...and his eyes are like the eyelids of the morning (Job 41:18).

The Leviathan spirit uses his eyes to monitor his prey and ascertain when his intended victim has entered a vulnerable position. When his prey is in a weakened state, Leviathan strikes. The surveillance he conducts is likened to observations made in the light of day, meaning his prey is exposed and cannot be hidden.

The Leviathan spirit also projects seduction, terror, and arrogance with his eyes or by his look (countenance). The Bible speaks of the eyelids that are lifted up.

> There is a generation, O how lofty are their eyes! and their eyelids are lifted up (Prov. 30:13).

In part through these projections, the Leviathan spirit is responsible for the vanity and pride manifested in those whom he influences or possesses.

His Tongue

> Canst thou draw out leviathan with a hook? or his tongue with a cord which thou lettest down? (Job 41:1).

The tongue of the Leviathan spirit is poisonous. A Leviathan-possessed personality will be marked by a venomous tongue full of lies, deception, gossiping, backbiting, slandering, destruction, and killing. The Bible speaks of a scourged tongue in the Book of Job:

Thou shalt be hid from the scourge of the tongue: neither shalt thou be afraid of destruction when it cometh (Job 5:21).

This Bible verse shows that the tongue has the power to inflict severe punishment, suffering, and affliction.

The Bible also speaks of a "viper's tongue," which is the tongue of the Leviathan spirit. When it strikes its prey, this tongue introduces poison that brings destruction and, eventually, death.

He shall suck the poison of asps; the viper's tongue shall slay him (Job 20:16).

The Bible speaks of a tongue that devises "mischiefs":

Thy tongue deviseth mischiefs; like a sharp razor, working deceitfully (Ps. 52:2).

A Leviathan-spirit-possessed personality will display this razor-sharp speech and become an agent of mischief, whether in the family or at home, at church or in the community.

The tongue of the Leviathan spirit is deceitful. He uses his deceitful tongue to program error into the minds of his targeted prey.

Thou lovest evil more than good; and lying rather than to speak righteousness. Selah. Thou lovest all devouring words, O thou deceitful tongue (Ps. 52:3-4).

His Mouth

The demon Leviathan releases burning lamps and sparks of fire from his mouth to cause spiritual and physical destruction.

Out of his mouth go burning lamps, and sparks of fire leap out (Job 41:19).

I believe that the burning lamps vomited out of the mouth of Leviathan are actually demons assigned to bring about specific evils such as perversion, oppression, and affliction (see Rev. 16:13). The sparks of fire and arrows of darkness are sent to cause confusion, disagreement, or even death among the people and churches Leviathan is assigned to attack.

I also believe that the Leviathan spirit was the principal demon released against Job to arrange the calamities that befell him

Job 41:21 says that a flame goes out of Leviathan's mouth. With the flame from his mouth, the Leviathan spirit is able to physically set things on fire.

While he was yet speaking, there came also another, and said, The fire of God is fallen from heaven, and hath burned up the sheep, and the servants, and consumed them; and I only am escaped alone to tell thee (Job 1:16).

The servant of Job who escaped death thought that the fire coming from heaven had been set by God. I believe the fire was actually ignited by the Leviathan spirit.

His Nose

From his nose, Leviathan releases smoke as though some great cooking vessel were releasing vapors from inside him.

Out of his nostrils goeth smoke, as out of a seething pot or caldron (Job 41:20).

Whenever this evil smoke is released against a personality, place, or thing, evil clouds are formed over the target. The smoke from Leviathan's nostrils creates evil clouds that hinder light and instill darkness. (Darkness is associated with death, failure, suffering, and sin; light is associated with, life, salvation, prosperity, wisdom, and justice.)

The evil clouds generated can be clouds of:
Hindrance

Failure
Shame
Limitation
Oppression
Confusion
Bewitchment

When a person experiences confusion, indecision, and agitation, whether in a dream and or in real life, it may be a sign that the Leviathan spirit is acting against him.

The smoke from the nostrils of the Leviathan spirit blocks vision. His attack from the nostrils can hinder revelation and make dreaming almost impossible. However, the evil clouds from Leviathan's nostrils can be scattered or moved away by the power of the Holy Spirit. These evil clouds can be swallowed by the clouds of God, if we ask as much in prayer and fasting.

The evil clouds Leviathan generates are counterfeits God's doing and power. Through the mouth of David in the Bible, the Holy Spirit reveals God's power to release smoke from *His* nostrils.

There went up a smoke out of [God's] nostrils, and fire out of his mouth devoured: coals were kindled by it (2 Sam. 22:9).

His Teeth

The Lord declares that Leviathan has powerful teeth fitted together to hold his prey tight and also to crush.

Who can open the doors of his face? his teeth are terrible round about (Job 41:14).

There is only one way to rescue prey from the grip of the teeth of the Leviathan spirit: the demon's jaw must be broken.

And I brake the jaws of the wicked, and plucked the spoil out of his teeth (Job 29:17).

The rod of God is used as the spiritual weapon to break the jaw of Leviathan (see Job 21:9).

26

Powers in the Breath, Heart, and Sneezes of the Leviathan Spirit

His Breath

Leviathan's breath inflames coals and scatters terror. Just as the breath of God gives life, the breath of the Leviathan spirit gives evil, terror, sorrow, and death.

The Spirit of God hath made me, and the breath of the Almighty hath given me life (Job 33:4).

His [Leviathan's] breath kindleth coals, and a flame goeth out of his mouth (Job 41:21).

His Heart

We have already seen the stony heart of Leviathan as revealed by the Lord. When this demon sets his heart to do evil, he does not turn back or repent; instead, he completes the evil act without mercy.

His heart is as firm as a stone; yea, as hard as a piece of the nether millstone (Job 41:24).

Therefore, when he possesses a person, he turns that person's heart into stone that is set against the truth. Even the rejection and lack of understanding of the ministry of deliverance by some ministers of the gospel is the work of Leviathan.

The unmitigated ruthlessness of Leviathan is evident in the Book of Job. The Sabeans and Chaldeans who were possessed to attack the servants of Job wickedly killed them before taking away the oxen, asses, and camels.

And there came a messenger unto Job, and said, The oxen were plowing, and the asses feeding beside them: and the Sabeans fell upon them, and took them away; yea, they have slain the servants with the edge of the sword; and I only am escaped alone to tell thee (Job 1:14-15).

27

While he was yet speaking, there came also another, and said, The Chaldeans made out three bands, and fell upon the camels, and have carried them away, yea, and slain the servants with the edge of the sword; and I only am escaped alone to tell thee (Job 1:17).

His Sneezes

The sneezing of Leviathan produces lightning. By this, Leviathan is able to engender fear in the heart of his prey. Whenever unrealistic fear is generated, Leviathan's activities may be suspected.

By his neesings a light doth shine, and his eyes are like the eyelids of the morning (Job 41:18).

His Body

*I will not conceal his parts, nor his power, **nor his comely proportion** (Job 41:12, emphasis added).*

The Lord speaks of the proportion of Leviathan's body, because it gives insight into his structure and into the intimidating power of his appearance. Leviathan's frame can tower over and stand against a person, thereby limiting the person's forward progress.

A brother shared with me a dream he'd had in which Leviathan's activities against his life were revealed. In the dream, the man saw a huge monster towering over him. The animal-like creature had a long tail, but did not resemble any single animal species he had ever seen or of which he was aware.

The monster bent over the man in such a way that the man was pinned on his back, able to see only Leviathan's chest. The man tried to touch the demon, but was restricted from doing so. His inability to move spoke to the reason the attack of Leviathan had been unleashed: it was designed, not to kill the man, but to constrain him.

This confinement to a fixed position was reflected in the man's personal life. The dream was the means by which the Holy Spirit revealed the reality of a demonic power standing against this gentleman's forward progress.

Although the Leviathan demon had achieved some of his aims in hindering the man's life, Leviathan is by no means assured of success against us. There is a way out from under the influence of this demon spirit: even the formidable monster can be resisted in prayer and fasting by the power of the Holy Ghost. The enemy *shall* flee (see James 4:7). Amen!

The brother who related his dream encounter with Leviathan later entered into serious spiritual warfare against this monster demon and received his deliverance! Praise the Lord!

His Body Scales

His scales are his pride, shut up together as with a close seal. One is so near to another, that no air can come between them. They are joined one to another, they stick together, that they cannot be sundered (Job 41:15-17).

Leviathan's scales are so tightly arranged, they serve as his armor. This covering cannot be easily penetrated. No wonder the Lord says in Job 41:26-29 that no manmade weapon can force the Leviathan to run:

The sword of him that layeth at him cannot hold: the spear, the dart, nor the habergeon. He esteemeth iron as straw, and brass as rotten wood. The arrow cannot make him flee: slingstones are turned with him into stubble. Darts are counted as stubble: he laugheth at the shaking of a spear (Job 41:26-29).

The Leviathan spirit is confident that human effort cannot threaten his pursuits and activities. I believe this attitude indicates to us that the Leviathan is a military chief in the kingdom of darkness.

Ordinary weapons bounce off the body of Leviathan. The "ordinary" weapons to which I refer are spoken words or prayers that are declared without the knowledge of Biblical truth. Words and prayers that are not empowered by the Holy Spirit are no more potent than ordinary, everyday speech. They serve instead as spiritual weapons in the hands of the unrighteous.

Only spiritual weapons that are given to us by the Lord and combined with Biblical knowledge can make the Leviathan spirit flee. In the presence of such weapons, he *will* flee. Praise the Lord!

The Most Wicked Power From the Waters and Seas

The Leviathan spirit attacks by projecting, assigning, and possessing.

The Leviathan spirit projects wickedness into lives and families and projects division into relationships and marriages. He projects disagreement and discontent into the holy places of fellowship.

The Leviathan spirit assigns wickedness as a means to afflict people. Most often, afflictions of poverty, sickness, failure, and conflict can be traced to the attack of Leviathan, especially when these assignments are sent against believers in Jesus Christ.

The Leviathan spirit wearies its targets and then crushes them. Through affliction, he suppresses glory and breakthroughs and causes crying to take the place of laughter.

The Leviathan spirit also possesses souls to accomplish destruction and killing. His goal in possession is to dominate and control. When he possesses the soul (which consists of the will, the mind, and the emotions), the soul and all its functions are taken over. Leviathan's wickedness and evil agendas are easily transmitted to the mind of the individual who is possessed.

Possession by the Leviathan spirit will turn a tender personality into a heartless one able to destroy or kill without remorse.

One of Leviathan's trademarks is pride. Job 41:34 says *"he beholdeth all high things: he is a king over all the children of pride."* The Leviathan spirit initiates all violent and pride-related activities and conflicts in families, homes, churches, cities, and countries.

Chapter 3

Recognizing Leviathan

We have discussed many aspects of the Leviathan spirit and we are learning how his characteristics and weapons serve to hinder people and suppress the advancement of God's kingdom.

The following list summarizes many of Leviathan's qualities:

1. He is a military chief in the water kingdom of darkness.
2. He is a principal demon that operates from the water against anything or anyone who is for God and His kingdom.
3. He is a principal enemy of God, His Church, and His people.
4. He is the principal violent persecutor of God's people.
5. He is a demonic strongman; he holds down God's people and purposes and does not lose his hold easily.
6. He is the anchor spirit of Jezebel, the controlling personality.
7. He is a great launcher of evil and wickedness against anything that stands for the true God.
8. Leviathan is a marriage-breaker, destiny-destroyer, and killer of good things (spiritual and physical). In a word, he is a *waster*.
9. He is the crooked serpent with a hook that strangulates mercilessly.
10. He is the piercing serpent; he has the power to penetrate secured places and to bite.

11. He is the sea dragon.

Symptoms of Leviathan's Attack Against

the Body of Christ

I want to make it clear that everything about Leviathan involves violence. He does not come gently against his targets. He comes forcefully and quickly. Therefore, unless a strong resistance (through prayer and fasting) is raised against him, his attack will be swift and marked by disastrous results.

The Leviathan spirit creates severe forms of interference in the affairs of the Body of Christ. The disunity and division in the Body of Christ are, to a large extent, the works of the Leviathan spirit.

Before He ascended into heaven, Jesus prayed for the unity of the Body of Christ (see John 17). He knew that, as soon as He left the natural realm, the spirit Leviathan would come against His body to cause disunity. The primary cause of this disunity is spiritual pride.

Leviathan's attack against the Church is complex and strategic. The first symptom of his attack is the manifestation of fear—sudden and unrealistic fear within the congregation.

Remember the Lord's disclosure in Job 41:18 that, by the Leviathan spirit's sneezing, a light shines. The light that shines implies lightning. This "lightning" occurring in the realm of the spirit creates fear wherever Leviathan attacks. This fear manifests in a variety of ways.

One form it takes is suspicion and distrust among members of the Body of Christ. Another form is found in dreams: the dreams of members of the body will be polluted. They will begin to have bad dreams about the Church as well as dreams against the leaders and each other.

Lying is another symptom of the Leviathan spirit's attack against the Church. Character assassination and exaggeration of church issues are manifested in Leviathan's wake. Destructive confrontations and accusations against leaders and other members become common. Words are manipulated to cause disaffection and disloyalty. Erroneous interpretation of the words coming from the pulpit is used to distort the message being preached.

Pride and self-centeredness are more symptoms of the Leviathan spirit's attack. These qualities lead to attempts to usurp power in the churches. These attempts occur at various levels of responsibility. There will be affronts and instances of disrespect shown to the leadership. These manifestations usually start with prominent personalities in the church and eventually spread throughout the church in order to breed disloyalty.

Little by little, fault-finding demons possess the souls of key helpers. Soon, baseless rumors are spread. It is at this point that the following condition described in the Word of God is seen in the church that is under Leviathan spirit's attack:

For where envying and strife is, there is confusion and every evil work (James 3:16).

The Leviathan spirit will attack the Church by causing strife. Then strife will bring about all kinds of evil work, ranging from backbiting to witchcraft.

Leviathan comes against the glory of the faithful in Christ. He is merciless in his attempts to destroy the blessings given by God to His people. Leviathan will initiate and enforce his stranglehold whenever he is given the opportunity.

Likely Targets for the Leviathan Spirit

All demons are opportunistic and strategic. Therefore, they choose their targets carefully for maximum impact. The following is a list of some of Leviathan's favorite targets:

1. Genuinely born-again people (they are marked by Leviathan for attack)
2. Those who, like Job, are committed or completely yielded to the living God, Creator of the heavens and the earth
3. Those with divine assignments to wage war against the hosts of darkness
4. Those who daily live in obedience to the living God
5. Those whose callings are destined to affect many souls
6. People who purpose to use their resources to build God's kingdom

7. Those who are prayerful
8. Those who are under curses, especially ancestral curses (The Leviathan spirit enforces curses.)

Leviathan Spirit's Attack Against Individuals

The attack of Leviathan on the individual depends upon the relationship that individual shares with the Lord. This includes the person's level of yieldedness and steadfastness. It also depends on the individual's divine assignment here on the earth.

A very prayerful brother shared with me a dream he had about the Leviathan spirit. In the dream, he was standing in a place not far from the seashore. Suddenly, a great wave raised the level of the water. The tide then overran the boundary of the shoreline, reached the man's location, and dragged him into the middle of the sea.

While he was amid the sea, a huge sea animal came up to him. The animal looked like a whale with a tail. It used its huge nose to throw the man up in the air. As soon as he landed, the whale-like animal threw him in the air again and again, until he awakened from the dream.

Leviathan's aim was to toss the man up and down until he submitted to the attack, thereby to be eventually crushed. Physically speaking, this brother had been going through a very tough time in his finances and marriage. The Leviathan spirit sought to make him weary so that he would stop praying and would instead seek help from another demonic agent. Then Leviathan would crush him.

Rather than giving in, however, this brother resisted and overcame the demon, by the power of the Holy Spirit. Praise the Lord!

O thou afflicted, tossed with tempest, and not comforted, behold, I will lay thy stones with fair colours, and lay thy foundations with sapphires (Isa. 54:11).

This is God's promise to those whom the Leviathan spirit troubles. Amen!

Prayer warriors, praying families, and praying churches can expect to face attacks from the Leviathan spirit. In his book, *Smashing the Hosts of Hell,* Pastor Win Worley of the Hegewisch Baptist Church writes: "When Leviathan manifests, expect a determined resistance to expulsion. He will often manifest with serpentine twisting and winding of the person's head, body and limbs."[1]

In that day the LORD with his sore and great and strong sword shall punish leviathan the piercing serpent, even leviathan that crooked serpent; and he shall slay the dragon that is in the sea (Isa. 27:1).

The Leviathan spirit is called the crooked serpent. The *American Heritage Dictionary* defines *crooked* as "having or marked by bends, curves, or angles" and "dishonest or unscrupulous; fraudulent."[2] The Leviathan spirit manifesting as a crooked serpent has the ability to wind and turn himself with great speed. He does this even as he holds a person; his sole aim is to cause the person to submit to him. He will also use his hook or tail to drag people along the path of destruction.

The Leviathan spirit manifesting as a piercing serpent attacks with his tongue, afflicting the feelings and senses of the person under attack. Leviathan projects evils with his eyes, penetrating the soul of his victim. This brings confusion into the mind of his prey. Once a person is debilitated in this way, Leviathan takes over the person's will.

A sister shared with me a dream she had about Leviathan during an attack against her church. In her dream, the head of a huge python emerged and protruded from behind the church altar. The python's head was very large. His two eyes rolled around as he shot out his long tongue.

As soon as people in the congregation saw the massive python, pandemonium broke out and people ran for their lives. This manifestation of the Leviathan spirit threw the church into disarray.

In the physical realm (not in the dream), three things later happened in that church:

1. First, members of the congregation began having bad dreams about each other, resulting in distrust among them.
2. Second, there arose rebellion in nearly all the departments of the church.

3. Third, many members stopped attending the church. When the pastor called to ask them why, they gave flimsy, incomplete, or insincere excuses for having left the congregation.

The Leviathan spirit is a ruthless opponent bent on the destruction of everything issuing forth from the kingdom of God. Although he is a precision fighter well-prepared for battle, the Leviathan spirit is no match for God!

Endnotes

1. Win Worley, *Smashing the Hosts of Hell*, (Highland, IN: Hegewisch Baptist Church, 1993), 15.

2. The American Heritage Dictionary, 3rd ed., s.v. "crooked."

Chapter 4

Divine Weapons to Defeat the Leviathan Spirit

Second Corinthians 10:4 says: *"The weapons of our warfare are not carnal, but mighty through God to the pulling down of strong holds…."*

God has thoroughly equipped us for battle. Therefore, when praying, believers can use the following divine weapons to subdue Leviathan and cause him to flee:

1. **The sword of the Lord:** This sword is a major weapon used by God against the Leviathan spirit (see Isa. 27:1). This sword is also used in prayer to avenge and bring judgment against the Leviathan spirit. Spiritually speaking, the sword of the Lord will cut Leviathan into pieces. This sword is used in prayer to cut off the wicked (see Ezek. 29:8; Judg. 4:15; Jer. 12:12).

    *In that day **the Lord with his sore and great and strong sword** shall punish leviathan the piercing serpent, even leviathan that crooked serpent; and he shall slay the dragon that is in the sea* (Isa. 27:1, emphasis added).

2. *The hook of the Lord: This spiritual weapon can be used in prayer to draw Leviathan out of his hiding place and bring him to judgment. The hiding place of Leviathan is his stronghold; therefore, prayers using the hook of the Lord are effective in dragging him out of the stronghold so that other weapons (such as the sword of the Lord) can be used against him. The hook of the*

37

Lord can also be used in prayer to send Leviathan back to where he came from (see Isa. 37:28-29).

3. **The blood of Jesus:** The blood of Jesus is used in prayer to nullify all legal grounds of attack by Leviathan and to overcome his onslaught. These legal grounds may have been established through personal sin, ancestral curses, evil covenants, etc. (see 1 John 1:7). Appropriating the blood of Jesus breaks the power of this demon spirit (see Rev. 12:11). The blood of Jesus is used in prayer to restore and repair damage done by the Leviathan spirit to the spiritual and physical life of an individual (see John 6:53). The blood of Jesus is also used in prayer to shield the believer from the vomit of the Leviathan spirit.

4. **The words of the Lord:** The words of the Lord are spirit and life (see John 6:63). When spoken against the Leviathan spirit in prayer, the words of the Lord work to accomplish whatever they were sent to do (see Isa. 55:11). Because the Leviathan demon has ears, he hears the words of the Lord and responds without resistance. Just as the altar responded to the words of the Lord spoken by the prophet of Judah (see 1 Kings 13:2,5), so also the wicked spirit Leviathan will obey.

   And he cried against the altar in the word of the LORD, and said, O altar, altar, thus saith the LORD... (1 Kings 13:2).

   O earth, earth, earth, hear the word of the LORD (Jer 22:29).

5. **The name of the Lord:** The Bible says that the name of the Lord is a strong tower into which the righteous can run for safety (see Prov. 18:10). The name of the Lord protects a believer who lives righteously from the violent attacks of Leviathan. The name of the Lord is used in prayer as a spiritual weapon of warfare and a defense against the attack of this demon spirit (see Ps. 20:1). In the name of the Lord, a believer can stand as an altar of prayer against

wickedness, after the example of the prophet Elijah at Mount Carmel (see 1 Kings 18:24,32).

6. **The finger of God:** This spiritual weapon is used in prayer to cast out Leviathan from his lodgings, his place of possession, or the place of his activities. The finger of God is also used in prayer to disgrace wicked powers.

But if I with the finger of God cast out devils, no doubt the kingdom of God is come upon you (Luke 11:20).

Then the magicians said unto Pharaoh, This is the finger of God: and Pharaoh's heart was hardened, and he hearkened not unto them; as the Lord had said (Exod. 8:19).'

7. **The power of the Holy Spirit:** A believer empowered by the Holy Spirit will be able to counter and neutralize the Leviathan spirit.

But ye shall receive power, after that the Holy Ghost is come upon you: and ye shall be witnesses unto me both in Jerusalem, and in all Judea, and in Samaria, and unto the uttermost part of the earth (Acts 1:8).

Behold, I send the promise of my Father upon you: but tarry ye in the city of Jerusalem, until ye be endued with power from on high (Luke 24:49).

How to Be Empowered to Overcome the Attack of Leviathan

The following godly characteristics empower us to prevail against the Leviathan spirit:

1. Genuine repentance of self-righteousness as demonstrated in the life of Job

Wherefore I abhor myself, and repent in dust and ashes (Job 42:6).

Repentance is an attitude of the heart. A heart that perceives its shortcomings and accepts them shall receive mercy from the Lord. Genuine repentance evokes God's grace and favor.

2. The determination to live in humility

    By humility and the fear of the LORD are riches, and honor, and life (Prov. 22:4).

    Without humility, a believer cannot go far in the things of the spirit. Humility is the key to spiritual power. The psalmist says the Lord hears the desire of the humble:

    LORD, thou hast heard the desire of the humble: thou wilt prepare their heart, thou wilt cause thine ear to hear (Ps. 10:17).

    The apostle Peter says God resists the proud, but gives grace to the humble (see 1 Pet. 5:5). A believer who lives in humility will receive the grace to overcome Leviathan's attack.

3. Total submission to the Lord, as seen in Job's life

    Then Job answered the LORD, and said, I know that thou canst do every thing, and that no thought can be withheld from thee. Who is he that hideth counsel without knowledge? therefore have I uttered that I understood not; things too wonderful for me, which I knew not (Job 42:1-3).

    Job understood that he lacked real knowledge of what had befallen him. He submitted to the Omniscient God, who knows all things. As believers, we must be very careful not come against Leviathan in our own power or our own limited knowledge.

4. Forgiveness and the willingness to pray for those who have wrongly accused or used us. This attitude was displayed by Job at the end of his trial.

*And the L*ORD *turned the captivity of Job, when he prayed for his friends: also the L*ORD *gave Job twice as much as he had before (Job 42:10).*

The people whom Leviathan uses against us need our forgiveness. The battle is not a physical one against people, but a spiritual one against powers, principalities, rulers of darkness, and spiritual wickedness in high places (see Eph. 6:12).

When the attitude of forgiveness is projected in our relationships with people, the Holy Spirit will empower us against the onslaught of the Leviathan spirit.

5. Being genuinely born again

But now being made free from sin, and become servants to God, ye have your fruit unto holiness, and the end everlasting life (Rom 6:22).

There is no compromise in this. Anyone who desires to counter Leviathan's attack must have accepted Jesus as Lord and Savior. Jesus must be Lord over our lives and over all that belongs to us. It is only on the basis of this grace that we can face the Leviathan spirit and overcome him.

6. Being filled with and empowered by the Holy Spirit

That he would grant you, according to the riches of his glory, to be strengthened with might [power] by his Spirit in the inner man (Eph. 3:16).

The Holy Spirit is the prevailing power behind a successful campaign against any principality or power. Therefore, it is very important to seek to be continually filled with the Holy Spirit. This is an ongoing process of waiting on the Lord in prayer and fasting. In this way, your spiritual horizons will be enlarged and strengthened.

7. Being willing to violently resist the Leviathan spirit in prayer and fasting

And he said unto them, This kind can come forth by nothing, but by prayer and fasting (Mark 9:29).

And from the days of John the Baptist until now the kingdom of heaven suffereth violence, and the violent take it by force (Matt. 11:12).

Demonic invaders are ejected only by force. That is how we recover the territory they have occupied. This is the reason our Lord Jesus made the hard statement that, from the time of John the Baptist, the gospel came through force. Anyone who desires to have the kingdom must take it violently.

This is true in both the physical and spiritual realms. Ask yourself these questions: Will a lazy person pray persistently? Will a procrastinator prove effective in life or in warfare? The answer is *no*. Prayer and warfare involve being active. Diligent pray-ers are willing to pay a price. When Jesus prayed in the Garden of Gethsemane, the Bible says that the sweat pouring from his skin fell as *"great drops of blood"* (Luke 22:44).

This is the very way in which Leviathan comes against men and women. He exerts himself. Therefore, those who desire to resist him must also be forceful, not in the flesh, but in the Spirit. It is through the power of the Holy Spirit that we resist the enemy.

What comes after the defeat of the fierce fighting demon called Leviathan is a sigh of relief and praises unto Almighty God. After the defeat of the Leviathan demon, health is restored to the sick; riches flow into the hands of the poor; supportive friends gather around those who were lonely; family members who once deserted the home return; broken relationship are restored; those denied promotion are lifted up; peace and unity come to homes, places of worship, families, communities.

When the Leviathan spirit is defeated, progress, fruitfulness, and multiplication attend all of our endeavors!

Chapter 5

Divine Power Over Demonic Forces

The Lord Jesus has given to us believers the power to deal with evil forces of oppression and affliction. He has deposited into us the overcoming power we need over demonic entities. He says in Luke 10:19:

> *Behold, I give unto you power to tread on serpents and scorpions, and over all the power of the enemy: and nothing shall by any means hurt you.*

The serpents and scorpions mentioned here are demonic beings. Our Lord Jesus Christ has given us power to tread upon them! Not only that, but He has also given to us His power to subdue *all* the power of the enemy, that is, of Satan, the adversary.

There is still more. Jesus Christ also gave us the **covenant insurance** that, *nothing,* not even the deadly Leviathan spirit will *by any means* hurt us. There is no means devised by the Leviathan spirit that can hurt us *if only we receive His power.*

The Leviathan spirit is a great enemy of the believer's peace. But our Lord and Savior has given us power over him. We are secured in Him. Hallelujah!

Believers also have a **covenant assurance** given to us by our Lord Jesus Christ, to counter demonic possessions. In the Gospel of Mark, Jesus says:

And these signs shall follow them that believe; in my name shall they cast out devils; they shall speak with new tongues (Mark 16:17).

To believers who opt to receive this covenant assurance and are ready to act on it, it shall be just as Jesus said—we shall cast out devils.

But according to the declarations of the Lord concerning the Leviathan spirit in Job 26:13, the monster was created to be a formidable spirit before the rebellion in heaven. And therefore the Leviathan spirit is among the kinds of demons that will not surrender easily unless fasting is added to our prayers. Through prayer and fasting we receive more of His power to deal with this kind of demon called Leviathan.

And when he was come into the house, his disciples asked him privately, Why could not we cast him out? And he said unto them, This kind can come forth by nothing, but by prayer and fasting (Mark 9:28-29).

When fasting is added to prayer, a lot more is spiritually accomplished. The spirit is strengthened and the Holy Spirit power within us is enlarged. Daniel speaks of his accomplishments in seeking God when he added fasting to his prayer.

And I set my face unto the Lord God, to seek by prayer and supplications, with fasting, and sackcloth, and ashes (Dan. 9:3).

And while I was speaking, and praying, and confessing my sin and the sin of my people Israel, and presenting my supplication before the LORD my God for the holy mountain of my God; Yea, while I was speaking in prayer, even the man Gabriel, whom I had seen in the vision at the beginning, being caused to fly swiftly, touched me about the time of the evening oblation. And he informed me, and talked with me, and said, O Daniel, I am now come forth to give thee skill and understanding (Dan. 9:20-22).

A believer who purposes to exercise his God-given authority and power against the Leviathan spirit must necessarily be empowered to do so by the Holy Spirit.

Apostle Paul says in Ephesians 3:16:

That he [the Lord] would grant you, according to the riches of his glory, to be strengthened with might [power] by his Spirit in the inner man….

The inner man needs to be strengthened with the power of the Holy Spirit before the believer can offer meaningful resistance to the onslaught of the Leviathan spirit.

How to Come Against the Leviathan Spirit in Prayer

A prayer warrior who desires to confront the Leviathan spirit must be spiritually and physically prepared.

To confront and defeat Leviathan, the blood of Jesus must be used as a weapon of protection, a spiritual shield to cover you during the time of prayer. Thanksgiving and praises must also be rendered to the Lord in acknowledgment of His power and faithfulness to deliver.

Praises unto the Lord bring deliverance. In the book of Acts, we see that when Paul and Silas sang praises to the Lord, an earthquake was generated. That earthquake brought deliverance:

And at midnight Paul and Silas prayed, and sang praises unto God: and the prisoners heard them. And suddenly there was a great earthquake, so that the foundations of the prison were shaken: and immediately all the doors were opened, and every one's bands were loosed (Acts 16:25-26).

Hymns are also powerful tools for the dismantling of demonic presences. I highly recommend that prayer warriors who want to confront Leviathan sing at least one hymn at the start of the prayer time against this formidable enemy.

Believers who choose to use the prayers included in this handbook must also choose a life of continuous sanctification. Leviticus 11:44 says:

For I am the Lord your God: ye shall therefore sanctify yourselves, and ye shall be holy; for I am holy...

To sanctify simply means to set apart, purify, and purge anything belonging to the devil (see John 14:30). To wage warfare against the Leviathan spirit, it is critical that we be in right standing with the Lord. Holiness, within and without, is required. Anything short of this may result in disaster, spiritually and physically.

As believers in the Lord Jesus Christ, we are sanctified by appropriating the blood of the Lamb of God. He is our holiness! We must also identify and revoke any and all legal ground previously ceded to the enemy. This is part of our sanctification process.

The prayers in this book are to be spoken aloud. We are addressing an entity that cannot read our minds, but hears the words we speak against him. Say these prayers aloud and speak them aggressively.

Consider this example: in Matthew 20:30-34, two blind men caused the Lord Jesus to stand still and attend to them:

And, behold, two blind men sitting by the way side, when they heard that Jesus passed by, cried out, saying, Have mercy on us, O Lord, thou son of David. And the multitude rebuked them, because they should hold their peace: but they cried the more, saying, Have mercy on us, O Lord, thou son of David. And Jesus stood still, and called them, and said, What will ye that I shall do unto you? They say unto him, Lord, that our eyes may be opened. So Jesus had compassion on them, and touched their eyes: and immediately their eyes received sight, and they followed him (Matt. 20: 30-34).

The Bible says they cried out twice, repeating the same words: *"Have mercy on us, O Lord, thou son of David"* (Matt. 20: 30). If they had kept their mouths shut after the first time, the story might not have ended the same way.

The same is true of the blind man, Bartimaeus, in the Gospel of Mark 10:46-52. He continued to say the same thing loudly until his cry caused Jesus to stand still.

The Bible even records the fact that Jesus' repeated His words in His time of prayer at Gethsemane:

And again he went away, and prayed, and spake the same words (Mark 14:39).

These are not what the Bible calls "vain repetitions" (see Matt. 6:7). Rather, they are genuine cries for solutions to contrary situations.

And he spake a parable unto them to this end, that men ought always to pray, and not to faint (Luke 18:1).

Jesus taught that we must face difficulties, not with resignation, but with prayer. This truth applies to the attacks of the demon spirit Leviathan. In order to overcome him, we must be insistent and persistent in prayer.

As mentioned earlier, to prevail, we must not only pray, but we must break the legal ground that we have given (whether knowingly or inadvertently) to the Leviathan spirit. These legal grounds provide Leviathan the right of attack against a person, family, marriage, church, business, and so on.

Legal ground is given to the enemy through ancestral curses and blood shedding, for instance. Breaking these platforms for Leviathan's attack is of great importance. Leaving these grounds in place will attract the demon spirit's attack, because he seeks to enforce and go beyond such curses.

Whatever the spiritual concerns we face, the primary means by which we undermine and overcome the enemy is by the blood of Jesus. With this in mind, let's proceed to prayer. We will begin by thanking the Lord for His blood and for the protection it provides.

Chapter 6

Thanksgiving and Protection Under the Blood

Our prayer journey is based in Scripture. For each prayer category, we will establish Bible Prayer Links; these are our foundations for effective prayer in each area of concern.

We will also establish areas of Prayer Focus to help us stay on track and pray through the situation effectively.

Finally, each prayer section will include Prayer Guides; these include specific instructions for the time of prayer and specific prayer points (including declarations) designed to dismantle the work of the Leviathan spirit.

We begin our journey in prayer by acknowledging the works, promises, and characteristics of the Almighty, and offering thanksgiving for all He is and does on our behalf.

✟ Prayers of Thanksgiving to the Lord

Bible Prayer Links

> *Offer unto God thanksgiving; and pay thy vows unto the most High: and call upon me in the day of trouble: I will deliver thee, and thou shalt glorify me (Ps. 50:14-15).*

> *Behold, I give unto you power to tread on serpents and scorpions, and over all the power of the enemy: and nothing shall by any means hurt you (Luke 10:19).*

And these signs shall follow them that believe; In my name shall they cast out devils; they shall speak with new tongues (Mark 16:17).

PRAYER FOCUS

- The giving of thanks to God as the first step in a prayerful encounter against the Leviathan spirit
- Understanding the importance of the offering of thanksgiving as one the Lord desires from believers

PRAYER GUIDES

1. Give thanks to the Lord in prayer for giving us the power to tread upon demonic powers (serpents and scorpions).
2. Give thanks to the Lord in prayer for giving us power over *all* the power of the enemy.
3. Give thanks to the Lord in prayer for the divine insurance that nothing shall by any means hurt us (believers).
4. Give thanks to the Lord in prayer for the divine assurance given to believers to cast out the devil in His name.
5. Give thanks to the Lord for His divine shield around us.
6. Give thanks to the Lord for His faithfulness to deliver us from evils.
7. Give thanks to the Lord for exposing the workings of our enemies to us, by the power of the Holy Spirit.

✝ Prayers Using the Blood of Jesus As a Weapon of Protection

Any believer, who purposes to use the prayers in this book to come against the Leviathan spirit, must use the blood of Jesus as a spiritual covering. This ensures being well-defended against any violent reactions from this terrible demon, until victory is achieved.

BIBLE PRAYER LINK

And they overcame him by the blood of the Lamb, and by the word of their testimony; and they loved not their lives unto the death (Rev. 12:11).

PRAYER FOCUS

- Using the blood of Jesus as the only legal ground by which we can assert that the Leviathan spirit cannot touch us
- Using the blood of Jesus as our security
- the blood of Jesus as our defense

PRAYER GUIDES

1. Sing hymns and render praises and worship songs to the Lord.
2. Pray words of thanksgiving to the Lord, for sustaining your life by His Spirit.
3. Let the cleansing power in the blood of Jesus blot out the sins and iniquities of past generations, in the name of Jesus (see 1 John 1:7).
4. Ask that, as you go into this battle against Leviathan, the Lord Jesus will soak you in His blood.
5. Cover yourself with the blood of Jesus from the attack of the Leviathan spirit, in the name of Jesus.
6. Declare: "I secure my life in the blood of Jesus."
7. Declare: "I secure my spirit, soul, and body in the blood of Jesus."
8. Declare: "I secure the lives of members of my household in the blood of Jesus."
9. Declare: "I secure my home, marriage, and family in the blood of Jesus."
10. Declare: "I secure the work of my hands in the blood of Jesus."
11. Ask that the blood of Jesus would shield you from the attack of the Leviathan spirit.

12. Ask for the protective power in the blood of Jesus to be evoked upon your life (including your marriage, your glory, your career), *now,* in the name of Jesus.

Next, we will direct our prayers as believers covered by the blood of Jesus and empowered to neutralize the siege of the Leviathan spirit.

Chapter 7

Neutralizing the Siege of the Leviathan Spirit

You have laid the foundation for your prayers by giving thanks to your Deliverer and acknowledging the power given to believers, especially the power inherent in the blood of Jesus.

The remaining chapters will provide additional prayer tracks to guide you to victory against the Leviathan spirit. You will find suggestions (in parentheses) designed to help you customize your prayers.

✟ **Prayers Using the Blood of Jesus As a Weapon of Battle**

BIBLE PRAYER LINKS

> *In that day the LORD with his sore and great and strong sword shall punish leviathan the piercing serpent, even leviathan that crooked serpent; and he shall slay the dragon that is in the sea (Isa. 27:1).*

> *And they overcame him* **[the Leviathan spirit and all forms of demonic oppression]** *by the blood of the Lamb, and by the word of their testimony; and they loved not their lives unto the death (Rev. 12:11).*

Prayer Focus

- Counterattacking the Leviathan spirit using the blood of Jesus
- Overcoming the Leviathan spirit's attack using the blood of Jesus
- Using the blood of Jesus to cut off Leviathan's interference in your life, ministry, and affairs

Prayer Guides

1. Sing hymns and render praises and worship songs to the Lord.
2. Give thanks to the Lord for sustaining your life by His Spirit.
3. Confess any known sin and plead the blood of Jesus.
4. Declare: "Let the cleansing power in the blood of Jesus blot out my sins and the iniquities of my past generations, in the name of Jesus" (see 1 John 1:7).
5. Pray: "Blood of Jesus, neutralize all legal grounds of attack being exploited by the Leviathan spirit in my life (job, marital destiny, etc.), in the name of Jesus" (see Rev. 7:14).
6. Pray: "Blood of Jesus, arise in the power of your deliverance and neutralize every battle assigned by the Leviathan spirit against me (my career, my marriage, my destiny, etc.), in the name of Jesus."
7. Declare: "In the name of Jesus, I hold up the blood of Jesus against every violent attack coming from the Leviathan spirit against my life (ministry, marriage, etc.)."
8. Declare: "In the name of Jesus, and by the redeeming power in His blood, I break the yoke of restrictive bondages imposed over my life (ministry, spiritual growth, spiritual goals, prayer spirit, etc) by the Leviathan spirit" (see 1 Pet. 1:18-19).
9. Declare: "In the name of Jesus, I use the blood of Jesus to cut off the evil projections of the Leviathan spirit into my mind."

10. Declare: "Let the blood of Jesus flush out of my body the vomit brought up against me by the Leviathan spirit, in the name of Jesus."
11. Declare: "Let the blood of Jesus cleanse away any pollution sent by the Leviathan spirit to contaminate my spiritual vision, in the name of Jesus."
12. Declare: "Let the blood of Jesus arise in the power of His divine protection and shield me and the members of my household from the warfare raised by the Leviathan spirit, in the name of Jesus."
13. Pray: "Blood of Jesus, arise in your overcoming power and still the violent warfare coming against my life (my marriage, my career, my job, etc.) from the Leviathan spirit, in the name of Jesus" (see Rev. 12:11).
14. Pray: "Blood of Jesus, arise in your overcoming power and overrule every accusation brought against me by the demonic powers of the water, in the name of Jesus" (see Rev. 12:11).
15. Declare: "Let the speaking voice of the blood of Jesus silence any demonic voice speaking contrary to my divine purpose in life" (see Heb. 12:24).
16. Declare: "Let the sacrificial blood of Jesus neutralize all generational curses operating in my life against my advancement, in the name of Jesus."
17. Declare: "Let the sacrificial blood of Jesus break all the covenants of darkness that are holding my life in bondage, in the name of Jesus."
18. Pray: "Thank You Jesus, for Your sacrificial and overcoming blood."

✞ **Prayers to Attack the Stronghold of the Leviathan Spirit and Slay Him**

Pastor Dave Williams, in his book *The Miracle Results of Fasting*, writes the following about the enemy:

You can't deal with an enemy you don't recognize. Satan's [also Leviathan's] work is undercover work; it is secretive, deceptive, and *hidden*.[1]

The hiding place of the Leviathan spirit must be uncovered. The searchlight of the Holy Spirit will pinpoint his hiding place. Once he is located, the weapons of the Lord will slay him.

BIBLE PRAYER LINKS

The strangers shall fade away, and be afraid out of their close places (Ps. 18:45).

When a strong man armed keepeth his palace, his goods are in peace: But when a stronger than he shall come upon him, and overcome him, he taketh from him all his armor wherein he trusted, and divideth his spoils (Luke 11:21-22).

A voice of noise from the city, a voice from the temple, a voice of the LORD that rendereth recompense to his ene- mies (Isa. 66:6).

In that day the LORD with his sore and great and strong sword shall **punish** *leviathan the piercing serpent, even leviathan that crooked serpent; and he shall slay the dragon that is in the sea (Isa. 27:1, emphasis added).*

Punish in the above verse can be translated "visit" or "avenge."[2] Our Lord is the omnipresent God. He deals with the Leviathan spirit wherever believers are engaged in the battle against him.

The LORD also thundered in the heavens, and the Highest gave his voice; hail stones and coals of fire. Yea, he sent out his arrows, and scattered them; and he shot out light- nings, and discomfited them (Ps. 18:13-14).

PRAYER FOCUS

In this prayer program, we shall forcefully come against:
- The stronghold of the Leviathan spirit
- The secrets and the hiding place of the Leviathan spirit

PRAYER GUIDES

1. Sing hymns and render praises and worship songs to the Lord.
2. Give thanks to the Lord for sustaining your life by His Spirit.
3. Confess any known sin and plead the blood of Jesus.
4. Declare: "Let the cleansing power in the blood of Jesus blot out my sins and the iniquities of my past generations, in the name of Jesus" (see 1 John 1:7).
5. Pray: "O Lord, through the Holy Spirit, please expose the hiding place of the Leviathan spirit to me, in the name of Jesus."
6. Declare: "I receive Holy Ghost power to invade Leviathan's territory and conquer him, in the name of Jesus."
7. Declare: "I use the hook of the Lord to draw out Leviathan from his hiding place, in the name of Jesus."
8. Declare: "Let the voice of the Lord chase the Leviathan spirit out of his stronghold and let the sword of the Lord slay him, in the name of Jesus" (see Isa. 66:6).
9. Declare: "Let the lightning of the Lord go forth now into the stronghold of the Leviathan spirit to discomfit him, in the name of Jesus" (see Ps. 18:14).
10. Pray: "At Thy rebuke, O Lord, let the path of the Leviathan spirit (in my life, home, business, destiny, etc.) be discovered and destroyed, in the name of Jesus" (see Ps. 18:15).
11. Pray: "At Your blast, O Lord, let the stronghold of Leviathan be uncovered and shattered to pieces, in the name of Jesus" (see Job 4:9).
12. Pray: "O Lord, thunder in heaven and release hailstones and coals of fire upon the stronghold of the Leviathan spirit attacking me, in the name of Jesus" (see Ps. 18:13).
13. Pray: "Thank You, Jesus, for giving me victory over the stronghold of the Leviathan spirit."

✟ Prayers to Dismantle the Siege of the Leviathan Spirit Against the Church

BIBLE PRAYER LINKS

In that day the LORD with his sore and great and strong sword shall punish leviathan the piercing serpent, even leviathan that crooked serpent; and he shall slay the dragon that is in the sea (Isa. 27:1).

No weapon that is formed against thee shall prosper; and every tongue that shall rise against thee in judgment thou shalt condemn. This is the heritage of the servants of the LORD, and their righteousness is of me, saith the LORD (Isa. 54:17).

And I say also unto thee, That thou art Peter, and upon this rock I will build my church; and the gates of hell shall not prevail against it (Matt. 16:18).

For evildoers shall be cut off: but those that wait upon the LORD, they shall inherit the earth (Ps. 37:9).

The LORD also thundered in the heavens, and the Highest gave his voice; hail stones and coals of fire. Yea, he sent out his arrows, and scattered them; and he shot out lightnings, and discomfited them. (Ps. 18:13-14).

PRAYER FOCUS

- Breaking the power of the Leviathan spirit assigned to extinguish the fire of revival in the Church
- Destroying the ability of the Leviathan spirit to cause confusion in the Church
- Cutting off the influence of Leviathan asserted to draw the Church into unfruitful spiritual ventures
- Neutralizing the interference of the Leviathan spirit in praise and worship
- Restoring to the Church the power to glorify God in all things

PRAYER GUIDES

1. Sing hymns and render praises and worship songs to the Lord.
2. Give thanks to the Lord for His promises concerning the Church (see Matt. 16:18).
3. Confess any known church sin or spiritual errors and plead the blood of Jesus.
4. Declare: "Let the cleansing power in the blood of Jesus blot out the sins and iniquities of the leaders and members of this church (name the church), in the name of Jesus" (see 1 John 1:7).
5. Declare: "Let every hiding place of the Leviathan spirit in this church (name the church) be exposed now, in the name of Jesus."
6. Declare: "Let the sword of the Lord come against and slay the Leviathan spirit troubling this church, in the name of Jesus."
7. Pray: "O Lord, let Your blood cut off the evil projections coming from the nostrils of the Leviathan spirit against this church (name the church), in the name of Jesus."
8. Declare: "I/We overthrow the siege of the Leviathan spirit against this church (name the church), by the blood of the Lamb of God."
9. Declare: "Projections of prayerlessness coming from the Leviathan spirit against this church (name the church), be cut off now by the blood of Jesus."
10. Declare: "All wickedness assigned against this church (name the church) through the mouth of the Leviathan spirit, fail, in the name of Jesus."
11. Declare: "I/We neutralize the strike capability of the Leviathan spirit against this church (name the church) with the power of the Holy Ghost, in the name of Jesus."
12. Pray: "O Lord, by Your power, destroy weapons of the Leviathan spirit fashioned against this church (name the church), in the name of Jesus."
13. Declare: "Let Leviathan's weapons of destruction fashioned against this church (name the church) backfire against him, in the name of Jesus."

14. Declare: "Let the lightning of the Lord scatter the clouds of confusion and strife generated through the smoke of the nostrils of the Leviathan spirit over this church (name the church), in the name of Jesus."

15. Declare: "I/We hold up the blood of Jesus against every form (whether crooked serpent, piercing serpent, or water dragon) in which the Leviathan spirit comes against this church (name the church), in the name of Jesus."

16. Pray: "O Lord, thunder from Your throne in heaven and release hailstones and coals of fire upon the heads of the Leviathan spirit attacking this church (name the church), in the name of Jesus" (see Ps. 18:13).

17. Pray: "O Lord, let the smoke from Your nostrils swallow up the smoke projected from the nostrils of the Leviathan spirit to cause confusion and strife in this church (name the church), in the name of Jesus" (see Ps. 18:8).

18. Declare: "I/we hold up the blood of Jesus against the mouth of the Leviathan spirit through which evils are launched against this church (name the church), in the name of Jesus."

19. Pray: "Thank You, Jesus, for the victory You have given this church over the power of the Leviathan spirit."

Endnotes

1. Dave Williams, *The Miracle Results of Fasting* (Tulsa: Harrison House, 2004), 71.

2. Biblesoft's New Exhaustive Strong's Numbers and Concordance with Expanded Greek-Hebrew Dictionary (1994, 2003, 2006). CD-ROM. Biblesoft, Inc. and International Bible Translators, Inc. s.v. "paqad," (OT 6485).

Chapter 8

Foiling Leviathan's Strategy Against Churches and Ministries

At the close of Chapter 7, you were guided in prayer against the siege of Leviathan upon the Church. The final prayer segment of the chapter addressed broad categories of attack, such as the Leviathan spirit's weaponry, opposition to revival, and instigations of confusion.

Let's continue in targeted prayers to unravel the specific strategies and tactics of the Leviathan spirit against the organizational elements of the Body of Christ, and to bar his access.

✝ Prayers to Destroy the Activities of the Leviathan Spirit in the Church

BIBLE PRAYER LINKS

> In that day the LORD with his sore and great and strong sword shall punish leviathan the piercing serpent, even leviathan that crooked serpent; and he shall slay the dragon that is in the sea (Isa. 27:1).
>
> Canst thou draw out leviathan with a hook? or his tongue with a cord which thou lettest down? (Job 41:1).

When any one heareth the word of the kingdom, and understandeth it not, **then cometh the wicked one, and catcheth away that which was sown in his heart.** This is he which received seed by the way side *(Matt. 13:19, emphasis added)*

For ye have not received the spirit of bondage again to fear; but ye have received the Spirit of adoption, whereby we cry, Abba, Father *(Rom. 8:15)*.

Associate yourselves, O ye people, and ye shall be broken in pieces; and give ear, all ye of far countries: gird yourselves, and ye shall be broken in pieces; gird yourselves, and ye shall be broken in pieces. Take counsel together and it shall come to naught; speak the word, and it shall not stand: for God is with us. *(Isa. 8:9-10)*.

No weapon that is formed against thee shall prosper; and every tongue that shall rise against thee in judgment thou shalt condemn. This is the heritage of the servants of the LORD, and their righteousness is of me, saith the LORD *(Isa. 54:17)*.

And they overcame him by the blood of the Lamb, and by the word of their testimony; and they loved not their lives unto the death *(Rev. 21:11)*.

PRAYER FOCUS

In this prayer program, we shall crush the warfare raised by the Leviathan spirit to:

- Hinder the move of the Holy Spirit in the Church.
- Diminish the believer's ability to hear and discern by the Holy Spirit.
- Swallow the Word of God and prevent it from settling in the hearts of the people.
- Cause rebellion in the Church.
- Cause backbiting in the Church.
- Cause hard- and cold-heartedness in the Church.

PRAYER GUIDES

1. Sing hymns and render praises and worship songs to the Lord.
2. Give thanks to the Lord for sustaining the Church by His spirit.
3. Pray prayers of thanksgiving on behalf of the leadership of the Church.
4. Confess known sins or spiritual errors committed by the church; then plead the blood of Jesus.
5. Declare: "Let the cleansing power in the blood of Jesus blot out the sins and the iniquities of the leaders and members of this church (name the church), in the name of Jesus" (see 1 John 1:7).
6. Declare: "I use the sword of God to cut off the tail of the Leviathan spirit holding members of this church (name the church) and their blessings captive and I set them free, in Jesus' name."
7. Declare: "I use the sword of God to cut off the tail of the Leviathan spirit drawing people away from this church (name the church), in the name of Jesus."
8. Declare: "Let the sacrificial blood of Jesus neutralize the confusion projected against this church (name the church) by the Leviathan spirit, in the name of Jesus."
9. Declare: "Leviathan spirit, we resist you and your activities in this church (name the church) and we command you to flee, in the name of the Lord Jesus Christ" (see Eph. 4:27).
10. Declare: "All wickedness vomited into this church (name the church) by the Leviathan spirit, dry up, in the name of Jesus."
11. Declare: "By the blood of the Lamb of God, I break the power of evil dominion and control being exercised over this church (name the church) by the Leviathan spirit."
12. Pray: "Holy Fire of God, incubate our church (name the church) and hinder the Leviathan spirit from operating in it, in the name of Jesus."
13. Pray: "Holy Ghost Fire, scatter Leviathan's projections of hard- and cold-heartedness into the lives of

the members of this church (name the church), in Jesus' name."

14. Declare: "Personalities possessed by the Leviathan spirit to work as Jezebels in this church (name the church), be exposed and flee, in the name of Jesus."

15. Declare: "Leviathan-possessed personalities in this church (name the church) who counterfeit the tongue of the Spirit, be silenced, in the name of Jesus."

16. Declare: "I/We bind and cast out counterfeit expressions of prophecy and the word of knowledge in this church, in the name of Jesus."

17. Pray: "O Lord, let every authority established over this church by the Leviathan spirit be dismantled by the Fire of the Holy Ghost, in the name of Jesus."

18. Pray: "Thank You, Jesus, for giving us victory over the power of the Leviathan spirit in this church."

✝ Prayers to Eject the Leviathan Spirit From the Church

BIBLE PRAYER LINKS

As soon as they hear of me, they shall obey me: **the strangers shall submit themselves unto me.** *The strangers shall fade away, and be afraid out of their close places (Ps. 18:44-45, emphasis added).*

When any one heareth the word of the kingdom, and understandeth it not, then cometh the wicked one, and catcheth away that which was sown in his heart. This is he which received seed by the way side (Matt. 13:19).

But if our gospel be hid, it is hid to them that are lost: In whom the god of this world hath blinded the minds of them which believe not, lest the light of the glorious gospel of Christ, who is the image of God, should shine unto them (2 Cor. 4:3-4).

Let the high praises of God be in their mouth, and a two-edged sword in their hand; To execute vengeance upon the heathen, and punishments upon the people; To bind their kings with chains, and their nobles with fetters of iron; To execute upon them the judgment written: this honour have all his saints. Praise ye the LORD (Ps. 149:6-9).

Thou shalt also decree a thing, and it shall be established unto thee: and the light shall shine upon thy ways (Job 22:28).

And then shall that Wicked be revealed, whom **the Lord shall consume with the spirit of his mouth,** *and shall destroy with the brightness of his coming (2 Thess. 2:8, emphasis added).*

Canst thou draw out leviathan with a hook? or his tongue with a cord which thou lettest down? (Job 41:1).

And these signs shall follow them that believe; in my name shall they cast out devils; they shall speak with new tongues (Mark 16:17).

PRAYER FOCUS

- Ejecting Leviathan spirit from the place he loves to reside—the holy place
- Neutralizing the operation of the counterfeit power of the Leviathan spirit in the Church
- Binding and casting out of the counterfeiting spirits of Leviathan that have been vomited into the Church
- Stopping Leviathan from hindering the gospel
- Decreeing the exit of the Leviathan spirit from the Church
- Using the hook of the Lord to draw out Leviathan from the Church

PRAYER GUIDES

1. Sing hymns and render praises and worship songs to the Lord.
2. Give thanks to the Lord for sustaining the Church by His spirit.
3. Confess known sins or spiritual errors committed by the church; then plead the blood of Jesus.

4. Declare: "Let the cleansing power in the blood of Jesus blot out the sins and iniquities of the leaders and members of this church (name the church), in the name of Jesus" (see 1 John 1:7).
5. Declare: "I bind and cast out the Leviathan spirit from this church (name the church), by the power of the Holy Ghost."
6. Declare: "Let the blood of Jesus banish the Leviathan spirit from this church (name the church), in the name of Jesus."
7. Declare: "By the Word of the Lord which says that I shall cast out demons in His name, I command Leviathan and his associate spirits to depart from this church (name the church), in the name of Jesus."
8. Declare: "By the Word of the Lord which says that I shall cast out demons in His name, I drive away Leviathan and his associate spirits from this church (name the church) to the bottomless pit, in the name of Jesus."
9. Declare: "By the Word of the Lord which says that I shall cast out demons in His name, I bind Leviathan and his associate spirits with chains and fetters of iron of the Lord and cast them out of this church (name the church), in the name of Jesus."
10. Declare: "By the Word of the Lord which says that I shall decree a thing and it shall be established unto me; I decree that the Leviathan and his associate spirits must leave this church now (name the church) and never return, in the name of Jesus."
11. Declare: "Let the Fire of the Holy Ghost incubate this church now (name the church) and cast off any demonic presence, in the name of Jesus."
12. Pray: "O Lord, consume with the spirit of Your mouth the Leviathan spirit that is troubling the peace of this church (name the church), in the name of Jesus."
13. Declare: "I profess by the anointing of the Holy Spirit that as the Leviathan spirit leaves this church, his tail shall not be able to drag out any church member with him, in the name of Jesus."

14. Declare: "I use the hook of the Lord to draw out the Leviathan spirit from this church (name the church), in the name of Jesus."
15. Declare: "Let every authority established in this church (name the church) by the Leviathan spirit be dismantled by the Fire of the Holy Ghost, in the name of Jesus."
16. Declare: "Let every form of control exercised over this church by the Leviathan spirit be taken away by the power of the Holy Ghost, in the name of Jesus."
17. Pray: "Thank You, Jesus, for giving us victory over the Leviathan spirit in this church" (name the church).

✞ Prayers to Break the Restraining Power of the Leviathan Spirit Over Callings and Ministries

BIBLE PRAYER LINKS

In that day the LORD with his sore and great and strong sword shall punish leviathan the piercing serpent, even leviathan that crooked serpent; and he shall slay the dragon that is in the sea (Isa. 27:1).

Thus saith the LORD, the Holy One of Israel, and his Maker, Ask me of things to come concerning my sons, and concerning the work of my hands command ye me (Isa. 45:11).

O love the LORD, all ye his saints: for the LORD preserveth the faithful, and plentifully rewardeth the proud doer (Ps. 31:23).

No weapon that is formed against thee shall prosper; and every tongue that shall rise against thee in judgment thou shalt condemn. This is the heritage of the servants of the LORD, and their righteousness is of me, saith the LORD (Isa. 54:17).

PRAYER FOCUS

- Dealing with the violent activities of the Leviathan spirit against callings and ministries
- Breaking the hold of the Leviathan spirit over a calling or ministry
- Commanding the fulfillment of the will of the Lord concerning the Leviathan spirit, which is the work of His hands

PRAYER GUIDES

1. Sing hymns and render praises and worship songs to the Lord.
2. Give thanks to the Lord for sustaining your calling and ministry by His Spirit.
3. Confess any known sin and plead the blood of Jesus.
4. Declare: "Let the cleansing power in the blood of Jesus blot out my sins and the iniquities of my past generations, in the name of Jesus" (see 1 John 1:7).
5. Declare: "I speak to every vomited influence of the Leviathan spirit into my body, spirit, and soul that is causing spiritual weakness and prayerlessness: dry up now, in the name of Jesus."
6. Pray: "Holy Ghost Fire, strengthen me in my inner man to overcome the arrows of spiritual weakness sent by the Leviathan spirit, in the name of Jesus."
7. Declare: "I break the power of all evil dominion and control by the Leviathan spirit over my calling and ministry, in the name of Jesus."
8. Declare: "I come against and cast down the activities of the Leviathan spirit in my ministry, by the power of the Holy Spirit."
9. Declare: "I hold up the blood of Jesus against the constraining power of the Leviathan spirit and, by this, I begin to experience the move of the Holy Spirit in my ministry, in the name of Jesus."
10. Declare: "In the name of Jesus and by His blood, I come out of the demonic stranglehold being exerted upon my ministry by the Leviathan spirit."

11. Declare: "In the name of Jesus, I use the hammer of God to break the jaw of the Leviathan spirit that is holding the progress of my ministry in captivity."
12. Declare: "In the name of Jesus and by His blood, I bind the deceptions that are projected over my calling and ministry by the Leviathan spirit."
13. Declare: "In the name of Jesus and with His blood, I cut off the projections of failure stretched over my ministry by the Leviathan spirit."
14. Pray: "Holy Ghost Fire, I ask in the name of Jesus, that You dismantle the demonic oppression set up over my calling and ministry by the Leviathan spirit."
15. Pray: "Awake, awake, put on strength, O arm of the LORD and break to pieces the restraining power of the Leviathan spirit over my life and ministry, in the name of Jesus" (see Isa. 51:9).
16. Declare: "With the blood of Jesus, I scatter the influence of the Leviathan spirit over my ministry."
17. Declare: "You foul power of the water that wants to swallow my divine purpose, be slain, in the name of Jesus."
18. Declare: "You foul Leviathan spirit opposing my divine ordination, I capture you with the hook of God and slay you with the sword of God."
19. Pray: "O Lord, let Your shadow cover my divine ordination to shield it from the attack of the Leviathan spirit, so that it may revive as the corn and grow as the vine, in the name of Jesus" (see Hosea 14:7).
20. Pray: "I thank You, Jesus, for giving me victory over the power of the Leviathan spirit."

✝ Prayers to Destroy the Attack of the Leviathan Spirit Against Ministerial Success.

BIBLE PRAYER LINKS

In that day the LORD with his sore and great and strong sword shall punish leviathan the piercing serpent, even leviathan that crooked serpent; and he shall slay the dragon that is in the sea (Isa. 27:1).

*And I prayed unto the LORD my God, and made my con-
fession, and said, O Lord, the great and dreadful God,
keeping the covenant and mercy to them that love him,
and to them that keep his commandments (Dan. 9:4).*

*No weapon that is formed against thee shall prosper; and
every tongue that shall rise against thee in judgment thou
shalt condemn. This is the heritage of the servants of the
LORD, and their righteousness is of me, saith the LORD
(Isa. 54:17).*

*And the LORD spoke unto Moses, saying, Phinehas, the
son of Eleazar, the son of Aaron the priest, hath turned
my wrath away from the children of Israel, while he was
zealous for my sake among them, that I consumed not the
children of Israel in my jealousy. Wherefore say, Behold,
I give unto him my covenant of peace: And he shall have
it, and his seed after him, even the covenant of an everlasting priesthood; because he was zealous for his God,
and made an atonement for the children of Israel (Num.
25:10-13).*

PRAYER FOCUS

- Casting down the projection of failure in the ministry by
  the Leviathan spirit
- Casting down the projection of spiritual pride by the
  Leviathan spirit
- Casting down the projection of prayerlessness by the
  Leviathan spirit

PRAYER GUIDES

1. Sing hymns and render praises and worship songs
   to the Lord.
2. Give thanks to the Lord for sustaining your life by His
   Spirit.
3. Confess any known sin and plead the blood of Jesus.
4. Declare: "Let the cleansing power in the blood of
   Jesus blot out my sins and the iniquities of my past
   generations, in the name of Jesus" (see 1 John 1:7).

5. Pray: "O covenant keeping God, arise in the might of Your power and slay the Leviathan spirit hindering my ministerial work, in the name of Jesus" (see Dan. 9:4).

6. Pray: "O Lord, let the wickedness of the Leviathan spirit come to an end in my ministry, in the name of Jesus" (see Ps. 7:9).

7. Pray: "Arise, O Lord in Your anger and slay the Leviathan spirit attacking the glory of my ministry, in the name of Jesus" (see Ps. 7:6).

8. Pray: "O Lord, illuminate the darkness created by the Leviathan spirit's smoke over my ministerial goals, in the name of Jesus" (see Ps. 18:28).

9. Pray: "O Lord, cause my spiritual lamp to be lighted and to glow, in the name of Jesus."

10. Declare: "Agents of darkness around me who are using Leviathan's power to oppress my ministerial success, the Lord rebuke you, in the name of Jesus."

11. Declare: "You Leviathan spirit, working against my ministerial success, manifest yourself and be paralyzed, in the name of Jesus."

12. Declare: "I receive from the Lord the covenant of an everlasting priesthood to excel in all my ministerial assignments, in the name of Jesus."

13. Declare: "O Leviathan, the Lord rebuke you! Get away from the path of my ministerial success, in the name of Jesus."

14. Declare: "Every roadblock established by the Leviathan spirit against my ministerial success, be dismantled now, by the power of the Holy Ghost."

15. Pray: "I thank You, Jesus, for giving me victory over the power of the Leviathan spirit."

Chapter 9

Defeating Leviathan's Strategy Against Spiritual Growth

The spirit of Leviathan, as motivated by Satan and the ways of the kingdom of darkness, seeks to impede spiritual growth on all levels. In this regard, spiritual warfare is personal—the enemy desires to squelch the personal relationship between man and God, by whatever means possible.

As blood-bought children of the King, we have authority in the name of Jesus to thwart the enemy's plans, cancel his "embargoes," and ensure our continued spiritual growth, to the glory of God!

✞ Prayers to Cancel Embargoes Imposed Upon Spiritual Growth by the Leviathan Spirit

According to Merriam-Webster, an *embargo* is, in the most general sense, a "stoppage, impediment," or "prohibition."[1] The Leviathan spirit seeks to stem spiritual growth by creating barriers and enforcing illegitimate prohibitions against our spiritual and physical progress as believers.

BIBLE PRAYER LINKS

In that day the LORD with his sore and great and strong sword shall punish leviathan the piercing serpent, even

leviathan that crooked serpent; and he shall slay the dragon that is in the sea (Isa. 27:1).

Another parable put he forth unto them, saying, The kingdom of heaven is likened unto a man which sowed good seed in his field: but while men slept, his enemy came and sowed tares among the wheat, and went his way (Matt. 13:24-25).

Give not sleep to thine eyes, nor slumber to thine eyelids. Deliver thyself as a roe from the hand of the hunter, and as a bird from the hand of the fowler (Prov. 6:4-5).

And the LORD spake unto Moses, Go unto Pharaoh, and say unto him, Thus saith the LORD, Let my people go, that they may serve me (Exod. 8:1).

No weapon that is formed against thee shall prosper; and every tongue that shall rise against thee in judgment thou shalt condemn. This is the heritage of the servants of the LORD, and their righteousness is of me, saith the LORD (Isa. 54:17).

PRAYER FOCUS

- Destroying any attacks of Leviathan designed to impede the study of the Word of God
- Destroying any attacks of Leviathan designed to hinder the believer's focus on spiritual goals and desires
- Cutting off the spirit of slumber projected by the Leviathan spirit to cause prayerlessness
- Coming against Leviathan's attempts to extinguish spiritual lamps
- Opposing Leviathan's attempts to hinder believers from moving in the Spirit
- Deactivating Leviathan's designs to shut out words of knowledge
- Derailing Leviathan's attempts to overshadow the spiritual gifts that operate in and through believers

PRAYER GUIDES

1. Sing hymns and render praises and worship songs to the Lord.
2. Pray words of thanksgiving to the Lord for sustaining your life by His Spirit.
3. Confess any known sin and plead the blood of Jesus.
4. Let the cleansing power in the blood of Jesus blot out the sins and iniquities of past generations, in the name of Jesus (see 1 John 1:7).
5. Declare: "By the blood of Jesus and in His name, I release the demonic stranglehold being exerted against my spiritual strength and power by the Leviathan spirit."
6. Declare: "In the name of Jesus, I use the sword of God to slash the backbone of the Leviathan spirit who seeks to weary me spiritually."
7. Declare: "I hold the blood of Jesus against every form of the Leviathan spirit that comes against me, in the name of Jesus."
8. Pray: "Holy Spirit, in the name of Jesus I ask that You frustrate every attempt (and every deception employed) by the Leviathan spirit to block my entrance into the Holy of Holies."
9. Pray: "O Lord, in the name of Jesus and by Your power which cannot be resisted, paralyze the power used by the Leviathan spirit to put out my spiritual lamp."
10. Declare: "In Jesus' name and with His blood, I neutralize all projections of prayerlessness sent against me by the Leviathan spirit."
11. Pray: "Lord Jesus, with Your blood, cut off all projections coming from the Leviathan spirit to make me spiritually unfocused and undisciplined."
12. Declare: "In the name of Jesus, I rebuke any spiritual deafness in my life caused by the Leviathan spirit."
13. Declare: "In the name of Jesus, I rebuke any spiritual blindness in my life caused by the Leviathan spirit."
14. Pray: "Holy Ghost Fire, release every word of knowledge captured by the Leviathan spirit and free me to move in the Spirit again, in the name of Jesus."

15. Declare: "You Leviathan spirit oppressing my spiritual gifts, the Lord rebuke you! Depart from me, in the name of Jesus."
16. Pray: "Holy Ghost Fire, in the name of Jesus, dismantle the spirit of slumber assigned against me by the Leviathan spirit."
17. Pray: "Thank You, Jesus, for giving me victory over the power of the Leviathan spirit."

✟ Prayers to Destroy the Veil of Spiritual Blindness and Deafness Fabricated by the Leviathan Spirit.

BIBLE PRAYER LINKS

In that day the LORD with his sore and great and strong sword shall punish leviathan the piercing serpent, even leviathan that crooked serpent; and he shall slay the dragon that is in the sea (Isa. 27:1).

And in that day shall the deaf hear the words of the book, and the eyes of the blind shall see out of obscurity, and out of darkness (Isa. 29:18).

Hear, ye deaf; and look, ye blind, that ye may see. Who is blind, but my servant? or deaf, as my messenger that I sent? who is blind as he that is perfect, and blind as the LORD'S servant? (Isa. 42:18-19).

Seeing many things, but thou observest not; opening the ears, but he heareth not (Isa. 42:20).

When Jesus saw that the people came running together, he rebuked the foul spirit, saying unto him, Thou dumb and deaf spirit, I charge thee, come out of him, and enter no more into him (Mark 9:25).

And these signs shall follow them that believe; In my name shall they cast out devils; they shall speak with new tongues; (Mark 16:17).

Prayer Focus

- Cutting off any projections of deafness and blindness from the Leviathan spirit
- Ejecting the spirit of deafness and blindness vomited by the Leviathan spirit
- Using the authority of the name of Jesus to bind and cast out blind and deaf spirits
- Destroying the veil of spiritual blindness and deafness

Prayer Guides

1. Sing hymns and render praises and worship songs to the Lord.
2. Pray words of thanksgiving to the Lord for sustaining your life by His Spirit.
3. Confess any known sin and plead the blood of Jesus.
4. Let the cleansing power in the blood of Jesus blot out the sins and iniquities of past generations, in the name of Jesus (see 1 John 1:7).
5. Pray: "O Lord, I ask in the name of Jesus that You scatter with Your lightning the smoke of the Leviathan spirit assigned to make me spiritually blind and deaf."
6. Declare: "By my authority in the third heaven, I cut off the projection of the Leviathan spirit sent forth to make me spiritually blind and deaf, in the name of Jesus" (see 2 Cor. 12:2).
7. Declare: "In the name of Jesus, I cast down the power of spiritual deafness and blindness assigned by the Leviathan spirit to lead me into spiritual error."
8. Declare: "Power of spiritual blindness and deafness energized by the Leviathan spirit, break and loose your hold in my life now, in the name of Jesus."
9. Declare: "Arrows of spiritual blindness and deafness sent forth to me by the Leviathan spirit, go back to your sender, in the name of Jesus."
10. Pray: "O Lord, let the blood of Jesus neutralize any evil blown out from the nostrils of the Leviathan spirit to cause spiritual blindness and deafness in my life, in the name of Jesus."

11. Declare: "By the Word of the Lord, I dismantle the power of spiritual blindness from my eyes and the power of spiritual deafness from my ears, in the name of Jesus."

12. Declare: "You power of spiritual blindness and deafness, the Lord rebuke you in my life, in the name of Jesus."

13. Declare: "By the word of prophecy, I command the power of spiritual blindness and deafness to break in my life.

14. Pray: "Lord Jesus, by the power of the Holy Spirit, destroy the veil of spiritual blindness covering my physical and spiritual eyes."

15. Pray: "Lord Jesus, by the power of the Holy Spirit, destroy the veil of spiritual deafness covering my physical and spiritual ears."

16. Declare: "Demons of blindness projected into my physical and spiritual eyes, I bind and cast you out, in the name of Jesus."

17. Declare: "Demons of deafness projected into my physical and spiritual ears, I bind and cast you out, in the name of Jesus."

18. Declare: "I speak to my spiritual eyes and say, 'Open by the power of the Holy Spirit and begin to see into the invisible realm, in the name of Jesus.'"

19 Declare: "I speak to my spiritual ears and say, 'Open by the power of the Holy Spirit and begin to hear the voice of the Holy Spirit, in the name of Jesus.'"

20. Declare: "O Leviathan spirit, the Lord rebuke you! Depart from me now, in the name of Jesus."

21. Pray: "Thank You, Jesus, for giving me victory over the power of the Leviathan spirit to cause spiritual blindness and deafness in my life."

✞ Prayers to Break the Limiting Power of the Leviathan Spirit Over Your Life

BIBLE PRAYER LINKS

In that day the LORD with his sore and great and strong sword shall punish leviathan the piercing serpent, even

leviathan that crooked serpent; and he shall slay the dragon that is in the sea (Isa. 27:1).

And the LORD spake unto Moses, Go unto Pharaoh, and say unto him, Thus saith the LORD, Let my people go, that they may serve me (Exod. 8:1).

Shall the prey be taken from the mighty, or the lawful captive delivered? But thus saith the LORD, Even the captives of the mighty shall be taken away, and the prey of the terrible shall be delivered: for I will contend with him that contendeth with thee, and I will save thy children (Isa. 49:24-25).

Behold, I give unto you power to tread on serpents and scorpions, and over all the power of the enemy: and nothing shall by any means hurt you (Luke 10:19).

No weapon that is formed against thee shall prosper; and every tongue that shall rise against thee in judgment thou shalt condemn. This is the heritage of the servants of the LORD, and their righteousness is of me, saith the LORD (Isa. 54:17).

PRAYER FOCUS

- Breaking the evil seal put in place by the Leviathan spirit to limit access to God's complete plan for your life
- Dismantling any form of evil establishment created by the Leviathan spirit

PRAYER GUIDES

1. Sing hymns and render praises and worship songs to the Lord.
2. Pray words of thanksgiving to the Lord for sustaining your life by His Spirit.
3. Confess any known sin and plead the blood of Jesus.
4. Let the cleansing power in the blood of Jesus blot out the sins and iniquities of past generations, in the name of Jesus (see 1 John 1:7).

5. Declare: "By the power in the blood of Jesus, I break the yoke of restrictive bondages over my life (my destiny, my prayer life, etc.), in the name of Jesus."

6. Pray: "O Lord, let the sacrificial blood of Jesus intercept and destroy all arrows of financial failure fired by the Leviathan spirit to my business (career, job, etc.), in the name of Jesus."

7. Pray: "O Lord, break the choking power of the Leviathan spirit over my spiritual and physical goals, in the name of Jesus."

8. Pray: "Holy Ghost Fire, destroy any dominion established by the Leviathan spirit over my life, in Jesus' name."

9. Declare: "I use the hook of the Almighty God to draw the Leviathan spirit out of my life, in the name of Jesus."

10. Declare: "No weapon of the Leviathan spirit fashioned against my life and destiny (my marriage, my relationships, etc.) shall prosper, in the name of Jesus."

11. Declare: "Every stubborn yoke assigned against me by the Leviathan spirit, I command you to break, by the blood of Jesus."

12. Declare: "Embargoes established against my glory by the Leviathan spirit, be removed by the power of the Holy Ghost and let my glory shine now, in the name of Jesus."

13. Pray: "O Lord, by the shadow of Your wing, keep me from the oppression of the deadly enemy Leviathan" (see Ps. 17:8-9).

14. Pray, "O Lord, in the name of Jesus, arise in Your power and neutralize the attack of Leviathan that is coming against Your purpose for my life."

15. Declare: "In the name of Jesus, I demolish with the explosive thunder of God, the wickedness launched against me from the water."

16. Declare: "By the Word of the Lord that calls me to be of good cheer, knowing that He has overcome the world (see John 16:33), I overcome the devices of the Leviathan spirit against my life and destiny, in the name of Jesus."

17. Declare: "I command any crocodile spirit that has swallowed my blessings to vomit them out now, in the name of Jesus."
18. Pray: "Thank You, Jesus, for giving me victory over the limiting power of the Leviathan spirit."

Endnote

1. *Merriam-Webster Online Dictionary, 2010,* s.v. "embargo," http://www.merriam-webster.com/dictionary/embargo (accessed March 29, 2010).

Chapter 10

Defeating Leviathan's Designs for Setback and Ensuring Breakthrough

The Christian life is a journey consisting of many decisions, events, seasons, and pathways. Taken together, they comprise the sum total of our life stories.

Spiritually speaking, faith in Jesus Christ leads us in the direction of breakthrough in all areas of our lives. These breakthroughs unleash destiny, glorify God, and thwart the kingdom of darkness. The Leviathan spirit therefore **seeks to deny our breakthrough and orchestrate setbacks.** His purpose is to keep us from being and doing all we were created to be and do.

As children of the Most High, we needn't accept the enemy's plans. Instead, we are called to cooperate with God (through prayer, spiritual warfare, and obedience) to defeat all demonic devices and live the abundant life Jesus died to provide for us.

The following prayers will guide you through the process of destroying the schemes of Leviathan to impede your progress (and the progress of others) in this life.

✞ Prayers to Lift Embargoes Imposed on Financial Breakthroughs by the Leviathan Spirit

BIBLE PRAYER LINKS

In that day the LORD with his sore and great and strong sword shall punish leviathan the piercing serpent, even

leviathan that crooked serpent; and he shall slay the dragon that is in the sea (Isa. 27:1).

Thou brakest the heads of leviathan in pieces, and gavest him to be meat to the people inhabiting the wilderness (Ps. 74:14).

And the LORD spake unto Moses, Go unto Pharaoh, and say unto him, Thus saith the LORD, Let my people go, that they may serve me (Exod. 8:1).

Then Isaac sowed in that land, and received in the same year a hundredfold: and the LORD blessed him (Gen. 26:12).

No weapon that is formed against thee shall prosper; and every tongue that shall rise against thee in judgment thou shalt condemn. This is the heritage of the servants of the LORD, and their righteousness is of me, saith the LORD (Isa. 54:17).

PRAYER FOCUS

- Lifting the embargoes imposed upon financial break-through by the Leviathan spirit
- Scattering every cloud of disfavor created by the Leviathan spirit
- Destroying the demon of Pharaoh assigned to enslave

PRAYER GUIDES:

1. Sing hymns and render praises and worship songs to the Lord.
2. Pray words of thanksgiving to the Lord for sustaining your life by His Spirit.
3. Confess any known sin and plead the blood of Jesus.
4. Let the cleansing power in the blood of Jesus blot out the sins and iniquities of past generations, in the name of Jesus (see 1 John 1:7).

5. Declare: "Every embargo imposed upon my prosperity by the Leviathan spirit, be removed by the power of the Holy Spirit, in the name of Jesus."
6. Declare: "Every embargo established in the heavenlies jointly by the Leviathan spirit and any ruling demon in my environment in order to block my open heaven, scatter, in the name of Jesus."
7. Pray: "O Lord, arrest with Your power all activities of the Leviathan spirit in my life."
8. Declare: "Every crocodile demon assigned against me and my blessings, be paralyzed, in the name of Jesus."
9. Declare: "By the blood of Jesus, I cut myself loose from the bonds of the Leviathan spirit."
10. Pray: "O Lord, in the name of Jesus, command the hosts of heaven to cast away the Leviathan spirit that chases beneficial people away from me."
11. Declare: "By my authority in the third heaven, I command the Leviathan spirit to vomit every blessing of mine that it has swallowed, in the name of Jesus" (see 2 Cor. 12:2).
12. Declare: "I overthrow every evil establishment set by the Leviathan spirit against my spiritual and financial breakthrough, in the name of Jesus."
13. Declare: "Any demon from the water assigned to arrest my divine wealth, be paralyzed, in the name of Jesus."
14. Declare: "By the blood of Jesus, I break any family curse that has drawn the Leviathan spirit to oppose my financial breakthrough."
15. Pray: "Thank You, Jesus, for giving me victory over the power of the Leviathan spirit."

✞ Prayers to Lift Embargoes Imposed on Ministerial Breakthrough by the Leviathan Spirit.

BIBLE PRAYER LINKS

In that day the LORD with his sore and great and strong sword shall punish leviathan the piercing serpent, even

leviathan that crooked serpent; and he shall slay the dragon that is in the sea (Isa. 27:1).

A man's pride shall bring him low: but honour shall uphold the humble in spirit (Prov. 29:23).

No weapon that is formed against thee shall prosper; and every tongue that shall rise against thee in judgment thou shalt condemn. This is the heritage of the servants of the LORD, *and their righteousness is of me, saith the* LORD *(Isa. 54:17).*

For, behold, I have made thee this day a defenced city, and an iron pillar, and brasen walls against the whole land, against the kings of Judah, against the princes thereof, against the priests thereof, and against the people of the land. And they shall fight against thee; but they shall not prevail against thee; for I am with thee, saith the LORD, *to deliver thee (Jer. 1:18-19).*

PRAYER FOCUS

- Breaking the power of the Leviathan spirit to strangulate ministerial experience and cause spiritual slumber
- Cutting off the projections of spiritual pride and self-centeredness sent by the Leviathan spirit
- Breaking the power of the Leviathan spirit to hinder entry into the realm of revelation and illumination by the Holy Spirit
- Removing blockages established by the Leviathan spirit to hinder entry into the most holy realm, where all needs are met supernaturally

PRAYER GUIDES

1. Sing hymns and render praises and worship songs to the Lord.
2. Pray words of thanksgiving to the Lord for sustaining your life by His Spirit.
3. Confess any known sin and plead the blood of Jesus.

4. Let the cleansing power in the blood of Jesus blot out the sins and iniquities of past generations, in the name of Jesus (see 1 John 1:7).

5. Pray: "O Lord, in the name of Jesus, let the sacrificial blood of Jesus intercept and destroy all arrows of failure fired at my ministry by the Leviathan spirit."

6. Declare: "Every embargo established against my ministerial progress and success by the Leviathan spirit, be shattered to pieces by the thunder of God, in the name of Jesus."

7. Pray: "Holy Ghost Fire, scatter, in the name of Jesus, every obstruction assigned against my spiritual vision by the Leviathan spirit."

8. Pray: "O Lord, arrest with Your power any and all activities of the Leviathan spirit in my ministry."

9. Declare: "By the blood of Jesus, I cut my ministry loose from the bonds of the Leviathan spirit."

10. Declare: "In the name of Jesus, I cut my prayer spirit loose from the bonds of the Leviathan spirit."

11. Declare: "By my authority in the third heaven, I command the Leviathan spirit to vomit every ministerial blessing of mine that he has swallowed, in the name of Jesus" (see 2 Cor. 12:2).

12. Declare: "Projections from the Leviathan spirit assigned to sap my spiritual strength, be cut off by the power of the Holy Spirit."

13. Pray: "Blood of Jesus, come against the activities of the Leviathan spirit in my ministry and destroy them, in the name of Jesus."

14. Pray: "O Lord, set Your eyes upon and destroy any and all means being used by the Leviathan spirit to block my ministerial breakthrough, in Jesus' name."

15. Pray: "O Lord, let Your glory overshadow my ministry for a fresh breakthrough, in the name of Jesus."

16. Declare: "I hold up the blood of Jesus against the constraining power of the Leviathan spirit and I experience the move of the Holy Spirit in my ministry, now, in the name of Jesus."

17. Pray: "Thank You, Jesus, for giving me victory over the power of the Leviathan spirit."

✞ Prayers to Nullify Projections of Ill Health by the Leviathan Spirit

Demonic attacks against your health are designed to refute the claims of the Cross, diminish your capacity to advance the Kingdom of God, and steal your faith.

As you pray, keep in mind the power of the blood of Jesus and the certitude of His covenant with us!

BIBLE PRAYER LINKS

In that day the LORD with his sore and great and strong sword shall punish leviathan the piercing serpent, even leviathan that crooked serpent; and he shall slay the dragon that is in the sea (Isa. 27:1).

*For **I will restore health unto thee, and I will heal thee of thy wounds,** saith the LORD; because they called thee an Outcast, saying, This is Zion, whom no man seeketh after (Jer. 30:17, emphasis added).*

*When the even was come, they brought unto him many that were possessed with devils: **and he cast out the spirits with his word, and healed all that were sick:** that it might be fulfilled which was spoken by Esaias the prophet, saying, Himself took our infirmities, and bare our sicknesses (Matt. 8:16-17, emphasis added).*

No weapon that is formed against thee shall prosper; and every tongue that shall rise against thee in judgment thou shalt condemn. This is the heritage of the servants of the LORD, and their righteousness is of me, saith the LORD (Isa. 54:17).

Heal me, O LORD, and I shall be healed; save me, and I shall be saved: for thou art my praise (Jer. 17:14).

And it came to pass on a certain day, as he was teaching, that there were Pharisees and doctors of the law sitting by, which were come out of every town of Galilee, and

Judaea, and Jerusalem: and the power of the Lord was present to heal them (Luke 5:17).

Have mercy upon me, O LORD; for I am weak: O LORD, heal me; for my bones are vexed (Ps. 6:2).

Bless the LORD, O my soul: and all that is within me, bless his holy name. Bless the LORD, O my soul, and forget not all his benefits: who forgiveth all thine iniquities; who healeth all thy diseases; (Ps. 103:1-3).

Who his own self bare our sins in his own body on the tree, that we, being dead to sins, should live unto righteousness: by whose stripes ye were healed (1 Pet. 2:24).

And in the morning, as they passed by, they saw the fig tree dried up from the roots. And Peter calling to remembrance saith unto him, Master, behold, the fig tree which thou cursedst is withered away. And Jesus answering saith unto them, Have faith in God (Mark 11:10-22).

He sent his word, and healed them, and delivered them from their destructions (Ps. 107:20).

Is any sick among you? let him call for the elders of the church; and let them pray over him, anointing him with oil in the name of the Lord: and the prayer of faith shall save the sick, and the Lord shall raise him up; and if he have committed sins, they shall be forgiven him (James 5:14-15).

PRAYER FOCUS

- Casting out the demon(s) assigned by the Leviathan spirit to uphold diseases and afflictions
- Restoring health to those afflicted by the Leviathan spirit
- Cutting off the evil projections from the Leviathan spirit that nourish diseases and sicknesses
- Destroying any poisons introduced into the body by the Leviathan spirit

PRAYER GUIDES

1. Sing hymns and render praises and worship songs to the Lord.
2. Pray words of thanksgiving to the Lord for sustaining your life by His Spirit.
3. Confess any known sin and plead the blood of Jesus.
4. Let the cleansing power in the blood of Jesus blot out the sins and iniquities of past generations, in the name of Jesus (see 1 John 1:7).
5. Declare: "Every projection of ill health coming from Leviathan against my body, spirit, and soul, be cut off by the blood of Jesus."
6. Pray: "O Lord, in the name of Jesus, let the sacrificial blood of Jesus intercept and destroy all arrows of ill health fired against me by the Leviathan spirit."
7. Declare: "Every evil assigned against my body by the Leviathan spirit, I shake you off, in the name of Jesus."
8. Declare: "By the power of the Holy Spirit and in Jesus' name, I break the hold of the Leviathan spirit upon my spinal cord."
9. Declare: "Every pain in my neck and shoulder region, receive healing now by the blood of Jesus."
10. Pray: "Holy Ghost Fire, flow as electric current through my body, choking and extinguishing any sickness and disease, in the name of Jesus."
11. Declare: "Demonic weapons of the Leviathan spirit assigned to bring and sustain pain in my spinal cord, decay now, in the name of Jesus."
12. Declare: "Sickness and disease (affliction) from the Leviathan spirit tormenting my body, receive the rebuke of the Lord. My body, be made whole, in the name of Jesus."
13. Say: "I declare with my authority in the third heaven that I am a citizen of heavenly Zion; therefore, no sickness or disease shall fasten itself to my body, in the name of Jesus" (see 2 Cor. 12:2).
14. Declare: "I destroy with the Fire of the Holy Ghost anything (any power or demon) that is giving life

to any disease in my body (cancer, diabetes, high blood pressure, etc.), in the name of Jesus."

15. Pray: "Lord Jesus, by the power of Your Word that dried up the unprofitable fig tree, let every sickness and disease in my body dry up and die so that my body may live in good health."

16. Pray: "Lord Jesus, by the power and authority of Your Word that dried up the unprofitable fig tree, let all tentacles of cervical cancer (or tuberculosis, etc.), dry up and die."

17. Declare: "Every sickness and disease in my body that is tied to iniquity, I break your power by the blood of Jesus."

18. Pray, "Thank You, Jesus, for giving me victory over the power of the Leviathan spirit."

✟ Prayers to Shield Our Youth From the Attacks of the Leviathan Spirit.

In every community, young people are the key to the future. The Leviathan spirit is aware of how precious our youth are, therefore, he seeks to derail their destinies.

Among Leviathan's strategies are attempts to lead our youth away from godly standards *and* hinder their education. As Pastor Win Worley of the Hegewisch Baptist Church explains in his book, *Smashing the Hosts of Hell*: "Leviathan works in causing learning difficulties for youngsters, including reading."[1]

The demonic power's desire is to lead young people in paths of destruction, by whatever means possible. Nevertheless, we have been given authority to stand in the gap for our youth and to ensure that their God-given destinies are fulfilled!

BIBLE PRAYER LINKS

In that day the LORD with his sore and great and strong sword shall punish leviathan the piercing serpent, even leviathan that crooked serpent; and he shall slay the dragon that is in the sea (Isa. 27:1).

No weapon that is formed against thee shall prosper; and every tongue that shall rise against thee in judgment thou shalt condemn. This is the heritage of the servants of the L<small>ORD</small>*, and their righteousness is of me, saith the* L<small>ORD</small> *(Isa. 54:17).*

Our fathers have sinned, and are not; and we have borne their iniquities (Lam. 5:7).

And all thy children shall be taught of the L<small>ORD</small>*; and great shall be the peace of thy children (Isa. 54:13).*

Though hand join in hand, the wicked shall not be unpunished: but the seed of the righteous shall be delivered (Prov. 11:21).

PRAYER FOCUS

- Neutralizing demonic attacks designed to make learning difficult for young people
- Neutralizing demonic attacks that make education unappealing to young people
- Neutralizing attacks from the Leviathan spirit designed to make children stubborn, disobedient, or rebellious
- Neutralizing attacks from the Leviathan spirit that pervert the destinies of children through the projection of negative, self-demeaning, or ungodly attitudes
- Breaking hold established over the lives of youths by the sins of the parents

PRAYER GUIDES

1. Sing hymns and render praises and worship songs to the Lord.
2. Pray words of thanksgiving to the Lord, for sustaining the lives of your children by His Spirit.
3. Confess any known sin and plead the blood of Jesus.
4. Let the cleansing power in the blood of Jesus blot out the sins and iniquities of past generations, in the name of Jesus (see 1 John 1:7).
5. Declare: "With the blood of Jesus, I cut off all projections by the Leviathan spirit of learning difficulties into the lives of my children."

6. Declare: "I reject all authorities of demonic powers over the lives and destinies of my children. I reject the right of demonic powers over the lives and destinies of my children. I reject the evil claims of ancestral powers over the lives and destinies of my children. I reject the influence of all contrary powers over the lives and destinies of my children, in the mighty name of Jesus Christ."

7. Declare: "Every projection of disobedience sent by the Leviathan spirit into the lives of my children (insert their names), I disconnect you now, in the name of Jesus."

8. Declare: "Demonic vessels of warfare established against the well-being of my children—scatter, in the name of Jesus."

9. Declare: "With the blood of Jesus, I cancel any legal ground from which the Leviathan spirit stands and seeks to keep my children from accepting Jesus Christ into their lives."

10. Declare: "Every stronghold established by the Leviathan spirit to counter the success of my children, be dismantled by the thunder of God, in the name of Jesus."

11. Declare: "Demonic power desiring to break the bond between me and my children, your tool shall turn against you, in the name of Jesus" (see Ps. 37:14-15).

12. Pray: "O Lord, create a new heart in each of my children, so that they can serve You for the rest of their days, in the name of Jesus."

13. Declare: "Powers from the water projecting disobedience and rebellion into the hearts of my children to turn them against me, be exposed and paralyzed, in the name of Jesus."

14. Pray: "Lord Jesus, fill the hearts of my children with Your love and truth, that they may reign with You now and in the world to come, in Your name" (see Rev. 20:6).

15. Declare: "By the Word of the Lord which says that the seed of the righteous shall be delivered, I release my

children from the hold of any spirits of disobedience and rebellion, in the name of Jesus."

16. Pray: "Father God, by the power and authority with which you decreed light to swallow darkness in the beginning, decroo obedience to swallow disobedience and submission to swallow rebellion in the lives of my children, in the name of Jesus" (see Gen. 1:3; John 1:5).

17. Pray: "Thank You, Jesus, for giving my children victory over the power of the Leviathan spirit and all other demonic entities."

Endnote

1. Win Worley, Smashing the Hosts of Hell, (Highland, IN: Hegewisch Baptist Church, 1993), 13.

Chapter 11

Loosing Bondages, Breaking Yokes, and Delivering the Possessed

Second Corinthians 2:11 declares that we are not ignorant of Satan's devices. We are empowered by God to remain spiritually attuned so that we can perceive and destroy all bondages and yokes of the enemy, including those of the demon Leviathan and his cohorts. We are also enabled by the Holy Spirit to cast out all demonic presences and set free the possessed, in Jesus' mighty name.

✟ Prayers to Loose the Bonds and Break the Yokes of the Leviathan Spirit

BIBLE PRAYER LINKS

And ought not this woman, being a daughter of Abraham, whom Satan hath bound, lo, these eighteen years, be loosed from this bond on the sabbath day? (Luke 13:16).

And he that was dead came forth, bound hand and foot with graveclothes: and his face was bound about with a napkin. Jesus saith unto them, Loose him, and let him go (John 11:44).

He looseth the bond of kings, and girdeth their loins with a girdle (Job 12:18).

No weapon that is formed against thee shall prosper; and every tongue that shall rise against thee in judgment thou shalt condemn. This is the heritage of the servants of the LORD, and their righteousness is of me, saith the LORD (Isa. 54:17).

For now will I break his yoke from off thee, and will burst thy bonds in sunder (Nah. 1:13).

For it shall come to pass in that day, saith the LORD of hosts, that I will break his yoke from off thy neck, and will burst thy bonds, and strangers shall no more serve themselves of him: (Jer. 30:8).

O LORD, truly I am thy servant; I am thy servant, and the son of thine handmaid: thou hast loosed my bonds (Ps. 116:16).

And it shall come to pass in that day, that his burden shall be taken away from off thy shoulder, and his yoke from off thy neck, and the yoke shall be destroyed because of the anointing (Isa. 10:27).

PRAYER FOCUS

- Breaking the restraining power of the Leviathan spirit, through the power of the Holy Spirit
- Setting free, in the name of Jesus, those held under the bonds of the Leviathan spirit
- Setting free those who have become deaf to the pleas of truth and reason
- Setting free the glory that has been caged by the enemy

PRAYER GUIDES

1. Sing hymns and render praises and worship songs to the Lord.
2. Pray words of thanksgiving to the Lord, for sustaining your life by His Spirit.
3. Confess any known sin and plead the blood of Jesus.

4. Let the cleansing power in the blood of Jesus blot out the sins and iniquities of past generations, in the name of Jesus (see 1 John 1:7).
5. Declare: "In the name of Jesus, I loose myself from the bonds of the Leviathan spirit."
6. Pray: "O Lord, I am your servant, the work of Your hand. In the name of Jesus, loose the bonds that Leviathan spirit has used to impede my progress."
7. Pray: "O Lord, in the name of Jesus, break off from me every stubborn yoke put upon me by the Leviathan spirit."
8. Declare: "Demonic bonds assigned to my hands to make me physically destitute, be untied and roast in the fire of God, in the name of Jesus."
9. Declare: "Demonic bonds assigned to my legs to confine me to the wrong place or position, I command you to be untied and to roast in the fire of God, in the name of Jesus."
10. Pray: "In the name of Jesus, let the anointing of the Holy Ghost break the yoke assigned to my destiny by the Leviathan spirit."
11. Declare: "Bonds of witchcraft assigned against my prosperity, break and loose your hold, in the name of Jesus."
12. Pray: "In the name of Jesus, let the rod of the Lord go forth and break the bonds of poverty assigned by the Leviathan spirit to the work of my hands (career, business, job, etc.)."
13. Pray, "In the name of Jesus, let the rod of the Lord go forth and break the bonds of sickness and disease assigned by the Leviathan spirit to afflict my body."
14. Declare: "By the power of the Holy Ghost I disconnect Leviathan's bonds set over my life to make me a non-entity in my generation, in the name of Jesus."
15. Declare: "By the word of prophecy in my mouth, I command the bonds of failure attached to my life (ministry, marriage, relationship) to fall apart and roast in the fire of God, in the name of Jesus."
16. Declare: "Bonds of affliction binding my glory with dishonor, break and fall apart, in the name of Jesus."

17. Pray: "O Lord, in the name of Jesus, burst asunder any bonds of the Leviathan spirit set upon my life."
18. Pray, "Thank You, Jesus, for giving me victory over the power of the Leviathan spirit."

✞ Prayers to Deal With Leviathan Spirit Possession

BIBLE PRAYER LINKS

And these signs shall follow them that believe; in my name shall they cast out devils; they shall speak with new tongues... (Mark 16:17).

But if I with the finger of God cast out devils, no doubt the kingdom of God is come upon you (Luke 11:20).

When the even was come, they brought unto him many that were possessed with devils: and he cast out the spirits with his word, and healed all that were sick: (Matt. 8:16).

Then was brought unto him one possessed with a devil, blind, and dumb: and he healed him, insomuch that the blind and dumb both spake and saw (Matt. 12:22).

And it came to pass, as we went to prayer, a certain damsel possessed with a spirit of divination met us, which brought her masters much gain by soothsaying:the same followed Paul and us, and cried, saying, These men are the servants of the most high God, which show unto us the way of salvation. And this did she many days. But Paul, being grieved, turned and said to the spirit, I command thee in the name of Jesus Christ to come out of her. And he came out the same hour (Acts 16:16-18).

Like a crane or a swallow, so did I chatter: I did mourn as a dove: mine eyes fail with looking upward: O LORD, I am oppressed; undertake for me (Isa. 38:14).

PRAYER FOCUS

- Binding and casting out any Leviathan spirit possession of an individual
- Binding and casting out any Leviathan spirit presence in an environment
- Binding and casting out any Leviathan spirit possession designed to undermine good projects
- Binding and casting out any Leviathan spirit possession designed to produce the works of high witchcraft against the life of God's servants through the spirit of Jezebel (see 1 Kings 18 and 19).

PRAYER GUIDES

1. Sing hymns and render praises and worship songs to the Lord.
2. Pray words of thanksgiving to the Lord, for sustaining your life by His Spirit.
3. Confess any known sin and plead the blood of Jesus.
4. Let the cleansing power in the blood of Jesus blot out the sins and iniquities of past generations, in the name of Jesus (see 1 John 1:7).
5. Declare: "Leviathan-possessed personalities that seek to undermine my physical and spiritual under-takings, be exposed and put to shame by the Holy Spirit, in the name of Jesus."
6. Declare: "Leviathan-possessed personalities that seek to counterfeit the power of God, be exposed and depart from me, in the name of Jesus."
7. Pray: "Lord, in the name of Jesus, let the power of the Holy Spirit separate me from Leviathan-possessed personalities assigned to demonically manipulate my life and destiny."
8. Pray: "O Lord, in Jesus' name and by Your power, expose agents of the Leviathan spirit that are gathered around me."
9. Pray: "O Lord, in Jesus' name and by Your power, expose agents of the Leviathan spirit that are in my environment."

10. Pray: "Let the sacrificial blood of Jesus deliver me, spirit, soul, and body, from the possession of the Leviathan spirit, in the name of Jesus."
11. Pray: "Holy Ghost Fire, block the route by which the Leviathan spirit would seek to possess my life (my children's lives, my spouse's life), in the name of Jesus."
12. Pray: "Let the Lord of Hosts undertake for me and deliver me from the oppressions of the Leviathan spirit, in the name of Jesus."
13. Declare: "In the name of Jesus, I refuse to be possessed by the Leviathan spirit to do wickedly."
14. Declare: "In the name of Jesus, I refuse to be possessed by the Leviathan spirit to go into errors."
15. Declare: "In the name of Jesus, I envelope my spirit, soul, and body with the Fire of the Holy Ghost against any Leviathan spirit possession."
16. Pray: "In the name of Jesus, let the finger of God cast the Leviathan spirit out of me (my children, my spouse) now."
17. Pray: "Thank You, Jesus, for delivering me from Leviathan spirit possession."

✝ Prayers to Break the Restrictive Bondages of the Leviathan Spirit.

BIBLE PRAYER LINKS

In that day the LORD with his sore and great and strong sword shall punish leviathan the piercing serpent, even leviathan that crooked serpent; and he shall slay the dragon that is in the sea (Isa. 27:1).

There go the ships: there is that leviathan, whom thou hast made to play therein (Ps. 104:26).

That [the LORD] strengtheneth the spoiled against the strong, so that the spoiled shall come against the fortress (Amos 5:9).

At Tehaphnehes also the day shall be darkened, when I shall break there the yokes of Egypt: and the pomp of her strength shall cease in her: as for her, a cloud shall cover her, and her daughters shall go into captivity (Ezek. 30:18).

No weapon that is formed against thee shall prosper; and every tongue that shall rise against thee in judgment thou shalt condemn. This is the heritage of the servants of the LORD, and their righteousness is of me, saith the LORD (Isa. 54:17).

PRAYER FOCUS

- Breaking the limiting power of the Leviathan spirit over businesses and careers
- Breaking every restriction imposed on success, progress, and breakthrough

PRAYER GUIDES

1. Sing hymns and render praises and worship songs to the Lord.
2. Pray words of thanksgiving to the Lord, for sustaining your life by His Spirit.
3. Confess any known sin and plead the blood of Jesus.
4. Let the cleansing power in the blood of Jesus blot out the sins and iniquities of past generations, in the name of Jesus (see 1 John 1:7).
5. Declare: "By the power in the blood of Jesus, I break the yoke of any restrictive bondage assigned by the Leviathan spirit over my life (ministry, calling, prayer life, etc.)."
6. Declare: "By the power of the Holy Ghost, I receive my liberty from any and all restrictions by the Leviathan spirit."
7. Declare: "You foul Leviathan spirit that seeks to limit the power of God in my life, the Lord rebuke you, in the name of Jesus" (see Ps. 78:41).

8. Pray: "In the name of Jesus, let the thunder of God strike and destroy any demonic walls erected by the Leviathan spirit against my progress."

9. Declare: "In the name of Jesus, I come against and pull down any demonic fortress established at the gate of my success and breakthrough by the Leviathan spirit."

10. Pray: "O Lord, in the name of Jesus, assign Your angels to pull down barriers set up against my advancement by the Leviathan spirit."

11. Pray: "O Lord, in the name of Jesus, paralyze the power of the Leviathan spirit that is supervising my confinement to an unfavorable condition."

12. Pray: "O Lord, in the name of Jesus and by Your power, break any yokes and dissolve any legal ground granting the Leviathan spirit dominion over my life (spirit, soul)."

13. Pray: "O Lord, let the pride of the power of the Leviathan spirit over my life come to an end, in the name of Jesus."

14. Declare: "By the Word of the Lord and in the name of Jesus, the gates of hell constructed by the Leviathan spirit against the glory of my destiny shall not prevail."

15. Pray: "Awake, awake, put on strength, O arm of the Lord and break to pieces the restraining power of the Leviathan spirit over my life and ministry, in the name of Jesus" (see Isa. 51:9).

16. Pray: "Lord Jesus, arise and defend Your interest in me."

17. Pray, "Thank You, Jesus, for giving me victory over the power of the Leviathan spirit."

Chapter 12

Countering All Forms of the Leviathan Spirit

In this chapter, we will pray specifically to quell the attacks by the Leviathan spirit in its various forms (as named in Scripture): the crooked serpent, the piercing serpent, and the dragon Leviathan.

✟ Prayers to Paralyze the Attack of the Crooked Serpent Leviathan

BIBLE PRAYER LINKS

In that day the LORD with his sore and great and strong sword shall punish leviathan the piercing serpent, even leviathan that crooked serpent; and he shall slay the dragon that is in the sea (Isa. 27:1).

By his spirit he hath garnished the heavens; his hand hath formed the crooked serpent (Job 26:13).

And the serpent cast out of his mouth water as a flood after the woman, that he might cause her to be carried away of the flood. And the earth helped the woman, and the earth opened her mouth, and swallowed up the flood which the dragon cast out of his mouth (Rev. 12:15-16).

No weapon that is formed against thee shall prosper; and every tongue that shall rise against thee in judgment thou shalt condemn. This is the heritage of the servants of the

LORD, *and their righteousness is of me, saith the* LORD *(Isa. 54:17).*

Behold, I give unto you power to tread on serpents and scorpions, and over all the power of the enemy: and nothing shall by any means hurt you (Luke 10:19).

And these signs shall follow them that believe; in my name shall they cast out devils; they shall speak with new tongues; they shall take up serpents; and if they drink any deadly thing, it shall not hurt them; they shall lay hands on the sick, and they shall recover (Mark 16:17-18).

But if I with the finger of God cast out devils, no doubt the kingdom of God is come upon you (Luke 11:20).

PRAYER FOCUS

- Destroying the choking power applied by the crooked serpent Leviathan against lives, marriages, careers, businesses, etc.
- Destroying the choking power applied by the crooked serpent Leviathan against the spiritual life (with the aim of obscuring the words of the Holy Spirit)
- Dismantling the demonic stranglehold of the crooked serpent Leviathan
- Uncoiling and straightening the crooked serpent Leviathan, so that the Holy Spirit operates freely among believers

PRAYER GUIDES

1. Sing hymns and render praises and worship songs to the Lord.
2. Pray words of thanksgiving to the Lord, for sustaining your life by His Spirit.
3. Confess any known sin and plead the blood of Jesus.
4. Let the cleansing power in the blood of Jesus blot out the sins and iniquities of past generations, in the name of Jesus (see 1 John 1:7).

5. Declare: "Crooked serpent spirit sent from inside the water to arrest me (my business, my marriage), be arrested and paralyzed by the Holy Ghost Fire, in the name of Jesus."

6. Declare: "Crooked serpent Leviathan assigned by Satan to kill me, be slain by the sword of the Lord, in the name of Jesus."

7. Declare: "Every crooked serpent Leviathan assigned to pursue me with intent to destroy, I command the ground to open up and swallow you now, in the name of Jesus."

8. Declare: "I receive Holy Ghost power to destroy the choking power of the crooked serpent Leviathan operating over my life (business, career, etc.), in the name of Jesus."

9. Declare: "By the blood of Jesus, I overcome the power of the demonic stranglehold exerted by the crooked serpent Leviathan over my life (my career, my business, etc.).

10. Pray: "O Lord, cause the strength of the crooked serpent Leviathan assigned to strangulate my physical and spiritual efforts to wither by Your power."

11. Pray: "Lord Jesus, arise in the might of Your power and liberate my life (destiny, soul, body, etc.) from the hold of the crooked serpent Leviathan."

12. Declare: "In the name of Jesus, I command any crooked serpent Leviathan present in my home (church, community, etc.) to uncoil and depart."

13. Pray: "O Lord, neutralize by Your blood, the evil effects issuing from the presence of the crooked serpent Leviathan (around me, my home, my family)."

14. Declare: "You crooked serpent Leviathan troubling my life (my family, my spiritual life, etc.), I command you in the name of Jesus to manifest and be paralyzed."

15. Pray: "Let the finger of God cast out the crooked serpent Leviathan from my environment (house, office, business office), in the name of Jesus."

16. Declare: "I hold the blood of Jesus against the constraining power of the crooked serpent Leviathan,

and I begin to experience progress in my life, in the name of Jesus."
17. Pray, "Thank You, Jesus, for giving me victory over the power of the Leviathan spirit."

✟ Prayers to Paralyze the Attack of the Piercing Serpent Leviathan

BIBLE PRAYER LINKS

In that day the LORD with his sore and great and strong sword shall punish leviathan the piercing serpent, even leviathan that crooked serpent; and he shall slay the dragon that is in the sea (Isa. 27:1).

At the last it biteth like a serpent, and stingeth like an adder (Prov. 23:32).

Their poison is like the poison of a serpent: they are like the deaf adder that stoppeth her ear; (Ps. 58:4).

And though they hide themselves in the top of Carmel, I will search and take them out thence; and though they be hid from my sight in the bottom of the sea, thence will I command the serpent, and he shall bite them: (Amos 9:3).

And the serpent cast out of his mouth water as a flood after the woman, that he might cause her to be carried away of the flood. And the earth helped the woman, and the earth opened her mouth, and swallowed up the flood which the dragon cast out of his mouth (Rev. 12:15-16).

No weapon that is formed against thee shall prosper; and every tongue that shall rise against thee in judgment thou shalt condemn. This is the heritage of the servants of the LORD, and their righteousness is of me, saith the LORD (Isa. 54:17).

Behold, I give unto you power to tread on serpents and scorpions, and over all the power of the enemy: and nothing shall by any means hurt you (Luke 10:19).

And these signs shall follow them that believe; in my name shall they cast out devils; they shall speak with new tongues; they shall take up serpents; and if they drink any deadly thing, it shall not hurt them; they shall lay hands on the sick, and they shall recover (Mark 16:17-18).

But if I with the finger of God cast out devils, no doubt the kingdom of God is come upon you (Luke 11:20).

PRAYER FOCUS

- Breaking the penetrating power of the piercing serpent Leviathan
- Neutralizing the effect of the sting of the piercing serpent Leviathan
- Blocking the route of the piercing serpent Leviathan
- Resisting the effort of the piercing serpent Leviathan to affect the senses and feelings
- Resisting the effort of the piercing serpent Leviathan to force his way into or through a family, a church, etc.

PRAYER GUIDES

1. Sing hymns and render praises and worship songs to the Lord.
2. Pray words of thanksgiving to the Lord, for sustaining your life by His Spirit.
3. Confess any known sin and plead the blood of Jesus.
4. Let the cleansing power in the blood of Jesus blot out the sins and iniquities of past generations, in the name of Jesus (see 1 John 1:7).
5. Declare: "Demonic power that has come from within the water and transformed into the piercing serpent in order to attack me, the Lord rebuke you, in the name of Jesus."

6. Pray: "Lord Jesus, arise in the might of Your power and liberate my spirit, soul, and body from the grip of the piercing serpent Leviathan."
7. Declare: "With the blood of Jesus and in His name, I completely barricade my senses from the sting of the piercing serpent Leviathan."
8. Declare: "With the blood of Jesus, I destroy any conscious or unconscious covenant that has given the piercing serpent Leviathan any legal ground to attack me."
9. Pray: "Let the blood of Jesus block every route the piercing serpent Leviathan desires to take in order to strike me, in the name of Jesus."
10. Pray: "O Lord, assign Your sword against the piercing serpent Leviathan who seeks to trouble my life. Slay him, Lord, in the name of Jesus."
11. Declare: "By the power of the Holy Ghost, I bind and cast out from my environment the piercing serpent Leviathan, in the name of Jesus."
12. Declare: "With the blood of Jesus, I neutralize the bite of the piercing serpent Leviathan."
13. Declare: "With the blood of Jesus, I cut off any evil projections from the piercing serpent Leviathan into my mind (family, relationship, etc.)."
14. Declare: "You foul, piercing serpent Leviathan attacking my glory, manifest and be paralyzed by the thunder of God, in the name of Jesus."
15. Pray: "Let the finger of God come against and disgrace the piercing serpent Leviathan that is attacking me, in the name of Jesus" (see Exod. 8:19).
16. Pray, "Thank You, Jesus, for giving me victory over the power of the Leviathan spirit."

✝ Prayers to Paralyze the Attack of the Dragon Leviathan

BIBLE PRAYER LINKS

In that day the LORD with his sore and great and strong sword shall punish leviathan the piercing serpent, even

*leviathan that crooked serpent; **and he shall slay the dragon that is in the sea** (Isa. 27:1, emphasis added).*

*Nebuchadrezzar the king of Babylon hath devoured me, he hath crushed me, he hath made me an empty vessel, **he hath swallowed me up like a dragon**, he hath filled his belly with my delicates, he hath cast me out (Jer. 51:34, emphasis added).*

Speak, and say, Thus saith the Lord GOD; Behold, I am against thee, Pharaoh king of Egypt, the great dragon that lieth in the midst of his rivers, which hath said, My river is mine own, and I have made it for myself (Ezek. 29:3).

But if I with the finger of God cast out devils, no doubt the kingdom of God is come upon you (Luke 11:20).

Then the magicians said unto Pharaoh, This is the finger of God: and Pharaoh's heart was hardened, and he hearkened not unto them; as the LORD had said (Exod. 8:19).

Thou didst divide the sea by thy strength: thou brakest the heads of the dragons in the waters. Thou brakest the heads of leviathan in pieces, and gavest him to be meat to the people inhabiting the wilderness (Ps. 74:13-14).

PRAYER FOCUS

- Dealing with the dragon Leviathan's swallowing power
- Recovering any blessings the dragon Leviathan has swallowed
- Dealing with the crocodile Leviathan

PRAYER GUIDES

1. Sing hymns and render praises and worship songs to the Lord.
2. Pray words of thanksgiving to the Lord, for sustaining your life by His Spirit.
3. Confess any known sin and plead the blood of Jesus.

4. Let the cleansing power in the blood of Jesus blot out the sins and iniquities of past generations, in the name of Jesus (see 1 John 1:7).

5. Declare: "You Leviathan spirit coming against me in the form of a dragon, the Lord rebuke you, in the name of Jesus."

6. Declare: "In the name of Jesus, I break the swallowing power of the dragon Leviathan and I command him to vomit every blessing of mine that he has swallowed."

7. Pray: "O Lord, cause Your finger to write a decree of judgment of death against the dragon Leviathan troubling my life (marriage, business, career), in the name of Jesus" (see Deut. 9:10).

8. Declare: "By my authority in the third heaven, I command the dragon Leviathan to vomit every blessing of mine that he has swallowed, in the name of Jesus" (see 2 Cor. 12:2).

9. Declare, "In the name of Jesus, I come against the dragon Leviathan with the finger of God and I cast him out into the desert place."

10. Declare: "In the name of Jesus and with the sword of the Lord, I cut off the many heads of the dragon Leviathan attacking my life (marriage, home, relationship, business)."

11. Pray: "O Lord, with Your hammer break the many heads of the dragon Leviathan by which wicked arrows are vomited against me to hurt me, in the name of Jesus."

12. Pray, "Thank You, Jesus, for giving me victory over the attack of the dragon Leviathan."

Chapter 13

Destroying the Attitudes, Lies, and Tactics of the Leviathan Spirit

As soldiers in the Kingdom of God, we are spiritually positioned (by the blood of Jesus, the name of Jesus, and the power of the Holy Spirit in prayer and declaration) to isolate demonic spirits and deactivate their devices.

✝ Prayers to Deal With Pride and Other Attitudes Engendered by the Leviathan Spirit

BIBLE PRAYER LINKS

[The Leviathan spirit's] scales are his pride, shut up together as with a close seal (Job 41:15).

[The Leviathan spirit] beholdeth all high things: he is a king over all the children of pride (Job 41:34).

When pride cometh, then cometh shame: but with the lowly is wisdom (Prov. 11:2).

Only by pride cometh contention: but with the well advised is wisdom (Prov. 13:10).

Pride goeth before destruction, and an haughty spirit before a fall (Prov. 16:18).

But when his heart was lifted up, and his mind hardened in pride, he was deposed from his kingly throne, and they took his glory from him (Dan. 5:20).

Notwithstanding Hezekiah humbled himself for the pride of his heart, both he and the inhabitants of Jerusalem, so that the wrath of the LORD came not upon them in the days of Hezekiah (2 Chron. 32:26).

Woe to the crown of pride, to the drunkards of Ephraim, whose glorious beauty is a fading flower, which are on the head of the fat valleys of them that are overcome with wine! (Isa. 28:1).

Every one that is proud in heart is an abomination to the LORD: though hand join in hand, he shall not be unpunished (Prov. 16:5).

PRAYER FOCUS

- Destroying any exaggerated opinion of self
- Dealing with any attitude of possessiveness
- Dealing with an unteachable attitude
- Dealing with judgmental attitudes

PRAYER GUIDES

1. Sing hymns and render praises and worship songs to the Lord.
2. Pray words of thanksgiving to the Lord, for sustaining your life by His Spirit.
3. Confess any known sin and plead the blood of Jesus.
4. Let the cleansing power in the blood of Jesus blot out the sins and iniquities of past generations, in the name of Jesus (see 1 John 1:7).
5. Pray: "O Lord, break me down and remold me to Your glory, in the name of Jesus."
6. Pray: "Blood of Jesus, intercept and destroy any arrows of pride fired against me by the Leviathan spirit, in the name of Jesus."

7. Pray: "Lord Jesus, depose from his kingly throne that Leviathan spirit assigned to destroy me, in the name of Jesus."

8. Pray: "O, Lord, as I confront the Leviathan spirit, let his crown of pride be trodden down, to your glory, in the name of Jesus" (see Isa. 28:3).

9. Pray: "O Lord, break the pride of the power of the Leviathan spirit troubling my life, in the name of Jesus" (see Lev. 26:19).

10. Declare: "In the name of Jesus, I bind and cast out of myself every unteachable spirit assigned to me by Leviathan."

11. Declare: "In the name of Jesus, I bind and cast out of myself or (name the persons) every judgmental spirit assigned by Leviathan."

12. Declare: "You dragon, Leviathan, with your mind hardened in pride against me or (name the person), I depose you from your kingly throne after the order of Nebuchadnezzar" (see Dan. 5:20).

13. Declare: "Crown of pride, sitting on my head or the head of (name the person) to draw me/us into error(s), I cast you away with the rod of God, in Jesus' name."

14. Declare: "Crown of pride, sitting on my head or the head of (name the person) to hold me/us in a state of spiritual passivity, I cast you away with the rod of God, in Jesus' name."

15. Declare: "Crown of pride, assigned to my head or the head of (name the person) by the Leviathan spirit to give me/us false security, I cast you away with the rod of God, in Jesus' name."

16. Declare: "Afflicting spirit of pride, I overcome you by the blood of Jesus."

17. Declare: "Poison of pride breathed on me or (name the person) by the Leviathan spirit, dry up, in the name of Jesus."

18. Declare: "In the name of Jesus, I command the poison of pride vomited up by the Leviathan spirit into the heart of (name the person) to evaporate."

19. Pray, "Thank You, Jesus, for giving me victory over pride."

✟ Prayers to Overthrow the Tongue of Lies Initiated by the Leviathan Spirit

Bible Prayer Links

Canst thou draw out leviathan with an hook? or his tongue with a cord which thou lettest down? (Job 41:1).

*But the king shall rejoice in God; every one that sweareth by him shall glory: **but the mouth of them that speak lies shall be stopped** (Ps. 63:11, emphasis added).*

*No weapon that is formed against thee shall prosper; **and every tongue that shall rise against thee in judgment thou shalt condemn**. This is the heritage of the servants of the* LORD, *and their righteousness is of me, saith the* LORD *(Isa. 54:17, emphasis added).*

Destroy, O Lord, and divide their tongues: for I have seen violence and strife in the city (Ps. 55:9).

Prayer Focus

- Silencing any lying tongues propelled by the Leviathan spirit
- Binding any lying tongue set against a person (church or family) by the Leviathan spirit

Prayer Guides

1. Sing hymns and render praises and worship songs to the Lord.
2. Pray words of thanksgiving to the Lord, for sustaining your life by His Spirit.
3. Confess any known sin and plead the blood of Jesus.
4. Let the cleansing power in the blood of Jesus blot out the sins and iniquities of past generations, in the name of Jesus (see 1 John 1:7).
5. Declare: "By the Word of the Lord (which declares that the mouths of liars shall be stopped), I command any lying tongues prompted by the Leviathan spirit to

speak against me (my ministry, etc.) to fall away, in the name of Jesus."

6. Declare: "By the Word of the Lord (which says that the mouths of liars shall be stopped), I overthrow every tongue prompted by the Leviathan spirit to speak lies against me (my ministry, etc.), in the name of Jesus."

7. Declare: "By the Word of the Lord (which says I shall condemn every tongue that rises against me in judgment), I rebuke every Leviathan-influenced tongue that is raised against my progress, in the name of Jesus."

8. Declare: "Leviathan, I bind your tongue, in the name of Jesus."

9. Declare: "Leviathan, I draw out your tongue with the cord of the Lord, in the name of Jesus."

10. Pray: "O Lord, in the name of Jesus and by Your power, stop the mouth of lies that is set against me."

11. Pray: "Holy Spirit my defender, arise and defend me from the tongues of men, in the name of Jesus."

12. Declare: "Every poison of lies spoken by the Leviathan spirit into the ears of (name the person), evaporate, in the name of Jesus.

13. Pray: "Thank You, Jesus, for giving me victory over the tongue of the Leviathan spirit."

✟ Prayers to Scatter Evil Clouds Generated by the Leviathan Spirit

BIBLE PRAYER LINKS

Out of his nostrils goeth smoke, as out of a seething pot or caldron (Job 41:20).

At Tehaphnehes also the day shall be darkened, when I shall break there the yokes of Egypt: and the pomp of her strength shall cease in her: as for her, a cloud shall cover her, and her daughters shall go into captivity (Ezek. 30:18).

With clouds he covereth the light; and commandeth it not to shine by the cloud that cometh betwixt (Job 36:32).

And the cloud of the LORD was upon them by day, when they went out of the camp (Num. 10:34).

Let God arise, let his enemies be scattered: let them also that hate him flee before him. As smoke is driven away, so drive them away: as wax melteth before the fire, so let the wicked perish at the presence of God (Ps. 68:1-2).

I saw in the night visions, and, behold, one like the Son of man came with the clouds of heaven, and came to the Ancient of days, and they brought him near before him (Dan. 7:13).

No weapon that is formed against thee shall prosper; and every tongue that shall rise against thee in judgment thou shalt condemn. This is the heritage of the servants of the LORD, and their righteousness is of me, saith the LORD (Isa. 54:17).

PRAYER FOCUS

- Scattering evil clouds assigned to waste
- Driving away evil clouds assigned to oppress and afflict
- Blowing away evil clouds ordained to bring or enforce captivity
- Commanding the clouds of the Lord to consume any evil clouds

PRAYER GUIDES

1. Sing hymns and render praises and worship songs to the Lord.
2. Pray words of thanksgiving to the Lord, for sustaining your life by His Spirit.
3. Confess any known sin and plead the blood of Jesus.
4. Let the cleansing power in the blood of Jesus blot out the sins and iniquities of past generations, in the name of Jesus (see 1 John 1:7).

5. Declare: "Evil clouds launched by the Leviathan spirit to hinder good things from coming to me, scatter and vanish, in the name of Jesus."
6. Declare: "Dark clouds assigned by the Leviathan spirit to cover the glory of my destiny, scatter and be cleared away, in the name of Jesus."
7. Declare: "Clouds of bewitchment over my life (marital destiny, business, career, etc.), scatter and be cleared away, in the name of Jesus."
8. Declare: "Any demonic power projecting clouds of failure and sorrow over my life (business, career, etc.), be paralyzed, in the name of Jesus."
9. Declare: "Any demonic power projecting clouds of stagnancy over my progress and advancement, be paralyzed, in the name of Jesus."
10. Pray: "Let the clouds of heaven overshadow me now, bringing divine revelation and power, in the name of Jesus."
11. Pray: "Father Lord, in the name of Jesus, assign Your thunder to scatter every cloud of oppression covering the works of my hand."
12. Pray: "O Lord, come in Your cloud and let Your glory fill my habitation for my sanctification, in the name of Jesus."
13. Pray: "O Lord, come in Your cloud and bless me, in the name of Jesus."
14. Declare: "Evil clouds generated by demonic agents to set me backward—scatter and vanish, in the name of Jesus."
15. Declare: "I command the Leviathan spirit projecting evil clouds over my life to be paralyzed, in the name of Jesus."
16. Pray: "Thunder of God, in the name of Jesus, scatter every evil cloud covering my destiny."
17. Pray: "Lord Jesus, let Your glory come as a cloud to consume any Leviathan spirit clouds hanging over my life."
18. Declare: "In the name of Jesus, I command any demonically ordained clouds hovering over my family to move away and never return."

19. Pray: "Thank You, Jesus, for giving me victory over the power of the Leviathan spirit."

Chapter 14

Breaking Ancestral Curses, Rebuking Leviathan, and Bringing Restoration

A s we come to the close of our prayer journey, it is fitting that we address the things of the past, present, and future.

The prayers in this final chapter will guide you in addressing and reversing ancestral curses of the past that are affecting your life today. They will also guide you in rebuking the present-day operation of the spirit Leviathan.

Finally, you will pray effectively, not only to undo the damage of previous attacks, but to restore your present condition to the will and Word of God, so that you can fulfill all the promise of your future in Christ!

✞ Prayers to Break the Ancestral Curses Leviathan Seeks to Reinforce

BIBLE PRAYER LINKS

*And now art thou cursed from the earth, which hath opened her mouth to receive thy brother's blood from thy hand; **When thou tillest the ground, it shall not henceforth yield unto thee her strength; a fugitive and a vagabond shalt thou be in the earth** (Gen. 4:11-12, emphasis added).*

*And Noah awoke from his wine, and knew what his younger son had done unto him. **And he said, Cursed be Canaan; a servant of servants shall he be unto his brethren** (Gen. 9:24-25, emphasis added).*

*And Jacob called unto his sons, and said, Gather your-selves together, that I may tell you that which shall befall you in the last days. Gather yourselves together, and hear, ye sons of Jacob; and hearken unto Israel your father. Reuben, thou art my firstborn, my might, and the begin-ning of my strength, the excellency of dignity, and the excellency of power: unstable as water, **thou shalt not excel**; because thou wentest up to thy father's bed; then defiledst thou it: he went up to my couch (Gen. 49:1-4, emphasis added).*

*And Isaac his father answered and said unto him, Behold, thy dwelling shall be the fatness of the earth, and of the dew of heaven from above; and by thy sword shalt thou live, **and shalt serve thy brother**; and it shall come to pass when thou shalt have the dominion, that thou shalt break his yoke from off thy neck (Gen. 27:39-40, emphasis added).*

*Behold, we are servants this day, and for the land that thou gavest unto our fathers to eat the fruit thereof and the good thereof, behold, we are servants in it: and it yiel-deth much increase unto the kings whom thou hast set over **us because of our sins**: also they have dominion over our bodies, and over our cattle, at their pleasure, and we are in great distress (Neh. 9:36-37, emphasis added).*

*Remember, O LORD, what is come upon us: consider, and behold our reproach. Our inheritance is turned to strangers, our houses to aliens. We are orphans and fatherless, our mothers are as widows. We have drunken our water for money; our wood is sold unto us. Our necks are under persecution: we labour, and have no rest. We have given the hand to the Egyptians, and to the Assyrians, to be satisfied with bread. **Our fathers have sinned, and are*** *not; and we have borne their iniquities (Lam. 5:1-7, emphasis added).*

PRAYER FOCUS

- Dismantling all hindrances and obstacles to current progress and advancement that have been established through the sins and iniquities of previous generations
- Breaking the power of any sicknesses and diseases tied to the sins and iniquities of previous generations
- Neutralizing the effects of ancestral curses resulting from evil covenants
- Neutralizing the effects of ancestral curses generated by past acts of wickedness

PRAYER GUIDES

1. Sing hymns and render praises and worship songs to the Lord.
2. Pray words of thanksgiving to the Lord, for sustaining your life by His Spirit.
3. Confess any known sin and plead the blood of Jesus.
4. Let the cleansing power in the blood of Jesus blot out the sins and iniquities of past generations, in the name of Jesus (see 1 John 1:7).
5. Declare: "Foundational curses afflicting my life and destiny, I loose your hold and break your power, in the name of Jesus."
6. Declare: "Every curse that has alighted upon my family line as a result of the sin of bloodshed, be broken and release me, in the name of Jesus."
7. Declare: "Any attack of the Leviathan spirit linked to any ancestral curse, be broken and nullified by the blood of Jesus."
8. Declare: "If my parents handed me over to any demonic power through any evil covenant, I call myself back now by the power of the Holy Spirit."
9. Declare: "Every ancestral curse of poverty afflicting me now, be broken by the blood of Jesus."
10. Declare: "With the blood of Jesus and in His name, I neutralize any affliction of sickness and disease in

my body that is tied to the sins and iniquities of my ancestors."

11. Declare: "Leviathan spirit assigned to supervise ancestral curses in my life, be paralyzed, in the name of Jesus."

12. Declare: "I break the power of and loose myself from all ancestral curses affecting my life and destiny, in the name of Jesus."

13. Declare: "By the blood of Jesus and the Fire of the Holy Ghost, I deliver my life and destiny from the grip of ancestral curses."

14. Pray: "Thank You, Jesus, for my deliverance."

☦ Prayers to Rebuke the Leviathan Spirit in the Name of the Lord

BIBLE PRAYER LINKS

Yet Michael the archangel, when contending with the devil he disputed about the body of Moses, durst not bring against him a railing accusation, but said, The Lord rebuke thee (Jude 9).

And the LORD said unto Satan, The LORD rebuke thee, O Satan; even the LORD that hath chosen Jerusalem rebuke thee: is not this a brand plucked out of the fire? (Zech. 3:2).

PRAYER FOCUS

- Coming against the Leviathan spirit, in the name of the Lord
- Rebuking the Leviathan spirit, in the name of the Lord
- Rebuking the activities of the Leviathan spirit, in the name of the Lord

PRAYER GUIDES

1. Sing hymns and render praises and worship songs to the Lord.

2. Pray words of thanksgiving to the Lord, for sustaining your life by His Spirit.
3. Confess any known sin and plead the blood of Jesus.
4. Let the cleansing power in the blood of Jesus blot out the sins and iniquities of past generations, in the name of Jesus (see 1 John 1:7).
5. Declare: "Leviathan, in whatever form you choose to manifest in order to disturb my peace, the Lord rebuke you, in the name of Jesus."
6. Declare: "Leviathan, in whatever form you choose to disguise yourself in order to attack me, the Lord rebuke you, in the name of Jesus."
7. Declare: "Leviathan, whatever the form you choose to take in order to possess any person and cause him/her to come against me, the Lord rebuke you, in the name of Jesus."
8. Declare: "Leviathan, the Lord rebuke you and all of your activities in my life, in the name of Jesus."
9. Declare: "Leviathan, regardless of any disguise you use to attack me, I uncover you by the power of the Holy Ghost and I slay you with the sword of the Lord, in Jesus' name."
10. Declare: "Leviathan, whenever you choose to come and oppose me, the lightning of the Lord shall strike you blind and force you to back away from me, in the name of Jesus."
11. Declare: "In the name of Jesus, I speak the rebuke of the Lord against any and all agendas of the Leviathan spirit to stagnate my life."
12. Declare: "In the name of Jesus, I speak the rebuke of the Lord against any weapons used by the Leviathan spirit to torment me."

✟ Prayers to Repair Damage Resulting From Leviathan's Attacks

BIBLE PRAYER LINKS

The hand of the LORD was upon me, and carried me out in the spirit of the LORD, and set me down in the midst of the valley which was full of bones, and caused me to pass by them round about: and, behold, there were very many in the open valley; and, lo, they were very dry. And he said unto me, Son of man, can these bones live? And I answered, O Lord GOD, thou knowest. Again he said unto me, Prophesy upon those bones, and say unto them, O ye dry bones, hear the word of the LORD. Thus saith the Lord GOD unto these bones; Behold, I will cause breath to enter into you, and ye shall live: and I will lay sinews upon you, and will bring up flesh upon you, and cover you with skin, and put breath in you, and ye shall live; and ye shall know that I am the LORD. So I prophesied as I was commanded: and as I prophesied, there was a noise, and behold a shaking, and the bones came together, bone to his bone. And when I beheld, lo, the sinews and the flesh came up upon them, and the skin covered them above: but there was no breath in them. Then said he unto me, Prophesy unto the wind, prophesy, son of man, and say to the wind, Thus saith the Lord GOD; Come from the four winds, O breath, and breathe upon these slain, that they may live. So I prophesied as he commanded me, and the breath came into them, and they lived, and stood up upon their feet, an exceeding great army (Ezek. 37:1-10).

PRAYER FOCUS

- Repairing—through the blood of Jesus, the power of the Holy Ghost, and words of prophecy—any damage done to believers' lives and destinies, marriages and homes, businesses and careers, etc., by the Leviathan' spirit
- Recovering the callings and ministries that have been damaged through the attack of the Leviathan spirit
- Reestablishing the glory of churches destroyed through the attack of the Leviathan spirit

PRAYER GUIDES

1. Sing hymns and render praises and worship songs to the Lord.
2. Pray words of thanksgiving to the Lord, for sustaining your life by His Spirit.
3. Confess any known sin and plead the blood of Jesus.

4. Let the cleansing power in the blood of Jesus blot out the sins and iniquities of past generations, in the name of Jesus (see 1 John 1:7).

5. Pray: "Blood of Jesus, begin to repair all damages done to my life through the attacks of the Leviathan spirit, in the name of Jesus."

6. Pray: "Blood of Jesus, begin to repair all damages done to my health through the poison of the piercing serpent Leviathan, in the name of Jesus."

7. Pray: "Blood of Jesus, begin to repair all damages done to my glory through the projections of the dragon Leviathan, in the name of Jesus."

8. Pray: "Blood of Jesus, bring together into one, the pieces of my soul that were fragmented through the attacks of the dragon Leviathan, in the name of Jesus."

9. Declare: "Damage done to my relationships through the oppression of the Leviathan spirit, be repaired now, in the name of Jesus."

10. Declare: "Projections of the Leviathan spirit assigned to abort my breakthroughs, be cut off with the blood of Jesus."

11. Declare: "Damage done to my marital destiny through ancestral demonic exchanges (pacts made with demons), be reversed now, in the name of Jesus."

12. Declare: "Damage done to my stomach, heart, kidneys, womb, or lungs by the poison of the piercing serpent Leviathan, be repaired now by the blood of Jesus."

13. Declare: "Perversions and diversions manifesting in my life and destiny as a result of the attacks of the Leviathan spirit, be neutralized now by Holy Ghost Fire, in the name of Jesus."

14. Declare: "By the word of prophecy, I command my fragmented soul to come together now, in the name of Jesus."

15. Declare: "By the word of prophecy, I command any divine potential that has been killed by the attack of the Leviathan spirit, to resurrect now, in the name of Jesus."

16. Declare: "All good things in my life that have been choked to death by the crooked serpent Leviathan, receive the resurrection power of the Lord Jesus Christ and come alive."

17. Declare: "Blessings that have been squeezed out of my life by the crooked serpent Leviathan, be recovered and restored now, in the name of Jesus."

18. Declare: "Let the bite of the piercing serpent Leviathan receive the blood of Jesus now and be healed, in the name of Jesus."

19. Declare: "In the name of Jesus, and by the power of the Holy Spirit, I recover all the blessings swallowed by the dragon Leviathan."

20. Pray: "Thank You, Jesus, for giving me total victory over the Leviathan spirit.

Conclusion

Occupy Until He Comes

In studying the spirit Leviathan and seeking to discern, disrupt, and destroy this demonic foe, we have taken to heart the admonition from Proverbs 4:7: *"Wisdom is the principal thing; therefore get wisdom: and with all thy getting get understanding."*

The Lord's revelation regarding this powerful foe has helped many people to grow in the wisdom and ways of God. You have read some of the testimonies of deliverance; there are many more. It is my firm belief that you, too, can experience the joys of a victorious life.

That is the reason this book was written. There is power in being equipped: no longer must we wonder how and why certain attacks are launched. Instead, we are positioned to watch and pray. We are wise to the tactics of this demon spirit, and aware of our role as the Army of God to oppose him in these last days.

Those who gain this understanding know the joys of standing in the gap and forcing back this fierce demon—not only for their own benefit, but on behalf of the Body of Christ. Individuals, intercessory teams, and even whole churches can pray these prayers aloud, lift their voices on behalf of one another; and share each other's experiences and testimonies.

Prayer by prayer and day by day, we are empowered to make headway in the direction of increased freedom, moving ever closer to the full manifestation of our covenant life in Christ! If we remain steadfast, we will gain more and more experience as victors and shed any remaining remnants of self-pity or victim mentality.

No longer will we be run over roughshod by Leviathan and his cohorts! This is not a season in which to be spiritually passive.

We are called to occupy our world until Jesus returns (see Luke 19:13). We are called to manifest the Kingdom of God in all things.

Therefore, it is not enough for us to know that someone somewhere is warring in this great battle. Instead, we must engage this enemy as a unified Body, each individual contending for the Kingdom, its people, and our God...each person lifting up others and being lifted up by them when the need arises...each believer having wisdom, knowledge, and understanding of the nature of the fight and being fully equipped to "*...overtake...and without fail recover all*" (1 Sam. 30:8).

To contact Joshua Tayo Obigbesan
Please write to:
P.O. BOX 110236
Aurora, CO 80042
or Email your prayer request to:
divinelibertyministries@yahoo.com

LaVergne, TN USA
03 October 2010
199355LV00003B/1/P